The College Teacher's Handbook:

A Resource Collection for New Faculty

MAGNA

Madison, Wisconsin

Magna Publications
2718 Dryden Drive
Madison, WI 53704
Magnapubs.com

The articles in this book have been previously published in *The Teaching Professor* and *Online Classroom* newsletters or have been adapted from Magna 20-Minute Mentor presentations.

ISBN: 978-0-912150-68-0

Contents

Foreword..5

PART 1 • Teaching Strategies...9
On Becoming a Teacher.. 10
Ten Things We Wish We Knew about Leadership before
    Stepping into the Classroom 13
Don't Waste the First Day 16
Skillful Teaching: Core Assumptions.................................... 18
Teaching as Storytelling 21
Four Ways to Teach More Effectively 23
Exploring What the Syllabus Communicates......................... 26
A Democratic Syllabus 29
It Makes a Difference When Teachers Care............................ 32
Assignments: How Students Perceive Them 35
Writing Good Assignment Descriptions................................. 38
Creating Effective Handouts 41
Successful Classroom Management 43
Taking Risks in Your Teaching 45

PART 2 • Student Learning..47
Reaching Students... 48
How Can I Communicate to Motivate and Engage my Students?...... 50
What Students Understand Isn't Always What the Professor Means .. 57
Questions: Why Do They Matter? 59
Group Work: Collaborative, Cooperative, or Problem-Based?............ 62
Designing Homework That Enhances Learning..................... 65
Three Tips for Navigating Contentious Classroom Discussions 67
Facilitating Discussion 70
Three Methods to Enhance Peer Review in Your Classroom 73
Student Presentations: Do They Benefit Those Who Listen?.............. 76
Writing Comments That Lead to Learning 78
Making the Review of Assigned Reading Meaningful 80
Helping Students Memorize: Tips from Cognitive Science 82

PART 3 • Testing and Evaluation..85
Does Dropping or Replacing the Lowest Exam Score Detract from
    Learning? 86
Testing That Promotes Learning 88
Making the Grading Process More Transparent 91

The Case for Reading Quizzes.. 94
The Value of Rubrics for Teachers 97
Using Evaluation Results to Improve: What Does It Take? 100
Grading Practices: More Subjective Than Objective? 104
Grading Advice: For Those Who Grade a Lot............................... 107
Cumulative Tests and Finals 110
Learning about Learning after the Exam... 112

PART 4 • Technology and Multimedia 115
Technology Policies: Are Some Better Than Others?...................... 116
Using Clickers Effectively: A Research-Based Tip........................... 118
An Analysis of PowerPoint-Based Lectures 120
PechaKucha and Ignite: Formats That Improve
    Student Presentations... 123
What Research Tells Us about Online Discussion 126
Are the Videos in Your Courses Promoting Learning? 129
Have You Considered Using Open Textbooks?................................ 132
Digital Content Curation.. 135
Creating Accessible Video for the Online Classroom...................... 137

PART 5 • Special Considerations 141
'100 Things Restaurant Staffers Should Never Do':
    Adapted for Teachers 142
Psychological Perspectives on Managing Classroom Conflict 145
The Day I Walked out of My Classroom 147
What Do I Need to Know About and Do for Students
    with Learning Disabilities? 149
Universal Design: What, How, and Why?....................................... 152
The Imposter with the Roster: How I Gave up Control
    and Became a Better Teacher 155

About the Contributors 157

Additional Resources 163

Foreword

Here's what I wish I'd gotten when I first started teaching: less advice. Everybody who has taught has advice for the new teacher. Some of it's good advice; some of it isn't, but when you're new and trying to get a handle on everything that needs to be done, you really don't have time to sort out the advice. What I wish I'd gotten (or been given) is a collection of material like this one. I started out teaching like many faculty still do—without any training, not much experience, but plenty of content knowledge. Truth be known, I taught for years without learning much of anything about teaching and learning beyond what I discovered while doing it.

And it is true. A lot of what you need to know about teaching can only be learned by teaching. But without any background knowledge, a good deal of what you learn first is discovered in the school of hard knocks. Most of us would have done much better in those first courses if we'd had a collection of resources like this one. These materials lay out the nuts and bolts of teaching—the activities, assignments, policies, and approaches that end up being what you do when you teach. What makes teaching fun, although in the beginning challenging might be a more apt description, is assembling from an array of possibilities your instructional approach. What you decide will make you unique—related to, but unlike any other teacher. What's not so easy is figuring out which decisions are best.

You want to make good decisions, but don't saddle yourself with needing to make the right decisions. Although we do know a lot about what makes instruction effective, those components can be executed in a host of different ways. And more important than being organized, clear, enthusiastic, and able to relate to students, is a collection of strategies and approaches that fit comfortably with who you are. They also must work well given the kind of content you teach, and they need to respond to the learning needs of the students you are teaching.

Yes, you can make wrong decisions. Chances are good you will make some; a lot of us make plenty. Most teachers don't start out all that impressively. You will be a better teacher the second time, third, and so on to some point where the instructional growth trajectory levels off. What makes for faster growth is viewing those decisions that turned out to be wrong or not very good as learning experiences—opportunities to understand some aspect of teaching and learning more fully. Growth as a teacher is inhibited if you let mistakes narrow the definition of what you can do and become as a teacher.

If you're taking a look at this book before you start teaching and are still in the process of deciding what you're going to do, trust your gut. If you read along and something strikes you as a good idea, something that you'd be comfortable doing or having students do, make a note of it. If you've already started teaching or have some teaching experience under your belt, then use the materials here to compare and contrast with the approaches you're using. There are two ways you can improve your teaching. You can do more of what's working and less of what isn't. To do either, you have to know your strengths and your weaknesses, and reading about what others do along with what the research recommends is a constructive way of encountering and developing your teaching self.

What's working well? What isn't? Those questions are straightforward, but the answers aren't. What's going well may be doing so part of the time or it's working well with some parts of the content or is helping some but not all students learn. And the same thinking applies when something doesn't work. Most things teachers try are not total failures. They work for a few students or they work, but just barely. New teachers are notorious for overreacting when things don't go smoothly. You won't be the first or the last teacher to make mistakes. It helps if you start out recognizing that learning to teach is a humbling experience—at least it was for most of us.

And that's another reason why a collection of materials on teaching and learning is such a valuable resource. So, something didn't work and although you may not have any idea about how to fix it, chances are good something's been written about other possibilities. And even if whatever you tried didn't work all that badly, others are using it differently and one of those ways just may be better. Teaching and learning can always be improved and reading is a great way to find out how.

Lots of books have been written for new teachers and some of them are excellent. The advantage of this book is that the articles are short. You can read the book from start to finish, but you can also read here and there, take a look at topics of interest, peruse those in areas where your knowledge is scant, and read carefully if it's an issue where you could use some help. The articles are free standing, so the content in one doesn't assume you've read the content covered in others. For those new to teaching, who need quick answers and easy to find information, it's a great collection. But you can take that with a grain of salt. Material I have a vested interest in is sprinkled throughout the collection.

Even though these are the twilight years of my career, I'm still teaching, still loving it, and still finding lots to learn about it. Start reading and just maybe you'll be feeling the love and finding out how much there is to learn about it.

Maryellen Weimer
April, 2018

PART 1

•

Teaching Strategies

On Becoming a Teacher

Maryellen Weimer, PhD

"'What is REAL?' asked the Rabbit one day. 'Does it mean having things that buzz inside you and a stick-out handle?'

"'Real isn't how you are made,' said the Skin Horse. 'It's a thing that happens to you. When a child loves you for a long, long time, not just to play with, but REALLY loves you, then you become Real . . . It doesn't happen all at once,' said the Skin Horse. 'You become. It takes a long time . . . Generally, by the time you are Real, most of your hair has been loved off, and your eyes drop out and you get loose in the joints and very shabby. But these things don't matter at all, because once you are Real you can't be ugly, except to people who don't understand.'"
— Margery Williams, *The Velveteen Rabbit*

The past three years have been a time of growth for me, some of it painful. I have become more humble and less arrogant. I have become less product-driven and more process-oriented. I have become less judgmental of my students' learning gaps and more engaged in helping them make up those gaps. I have learned not to teach to the middle just because most of my students are in the middle, but rather to challenge everyone to go beyond where they think they can go. I have taken more risks and been less afraid to make mistakes. I have learned to worry less about the students' perceptions of me and more about whether they understand what I am teaching. I have learned to let go of my preconceived ideas about students and to open myself to the surprises that each individual student has to offer.

I believe I have made a difference in the lives of my students, and I know they have made a difference in mine. Like the Skin Horse, I have learned that teaching isn't about shiny new technology or well-organized lesson plans impressively arrayed in a binder. Although these things help, teaching is really about being present for students and sharing with them the only thing we ultimately have to share, which is ourselves. Over the past three years, I have brought to my students all the reporting and writing skills I accumulated over nearly a 30-year career as a reporter. I've shared my passion for the craft, its important role in giving a voice to the voiceless, and a sense of the great adventures that await those who learn to practice it well. I hope I have also given them a new appreciation for the power and beauty of the English language and imbued in them a desire to write well, whether they are going into journalism or some other profession or simply writing for their own pleasure.

Among the lessons learned as I've worked to grow as a teacher is that the process of learning is often as important as the end product. For me, this is a radical change. As a journalist, all that mattered to my editors and me was getting the story, getting it right, and telling it in a compelling way. All eyes were on the story, not on what I might have learned in the process of doing it. When I first arrived at La Salle, I put a similar emphasis on the end product in my journalism classes. Even though I tried to take into account the place where students were starting, I focused almost exclusively on the quality of their stories, not on the process of their own development in getting the stories.

Today, however, I take as much pride in my students' sometimes halting efforts toward the goal as in their ability to reach the goal. The terribly shy student who, despite his fears, stands to read his story to the entire class is engaged in important learning. The Dominican student, who is writing in a second language, may not turn out the perfectly polished story, but she becomes an effective communicator when she pulls at our heartstrings by the tale she tells. The C student, who seems oblivious to much of what I teach, emails me after she has graduated to ask, "What was that Robert Frost poem you read to us on our last day? I really want to remember one line." While that student may not have produced the best work in the class, she took away from the class something important, even if it was that single line from Frost's poem.

I've also learned that my students tend to undervalue themselves, and one of the most important jobs I can do is to encourage them to be all they can be. A certain blue-collar mentality seems to pervade the student body— the idea that you're not supposed to be an intellectual or academically talented, so why even try? To address that, I've tried to expose students to the very best reporting and writing in America. I've also tried to give them more confidence in themselves, in the truth of their own experience, and in the power of expression. Some, miraculously, have responded. It has been truly wonderful to watch as students who never thought much about themselves have discovered, under my tutelage, that they have the potential to be excellent writers. "You mean this is really good?" "Yes, it's really good. And here's how you can make it even better."

Teaching at La Salle has given me, like the Skin Horse, a few more gray hairs. But it has also made me wiser and more real.

Reprinted from *The Teaching Professor,* May 2009

Ten Things We Wish We Knew about Leadership before Stepping into the Classroom

Laurie Bjerklie and Laura Mastel

We did it! We survived the application process, the grueling interviews, and the countless introductions. Finally, it was time to step into the classroom and share our passion and knowledge of medical laboratory science. We were ready to prepare students for associate degrees to become medical laboratory technicians, and we thought it would be easy. We had carefully prepared. Our textbooks were ready, our syllabi were done, and our labs were set up. What we found, however, were two teachers skilled in the area of laboratory medicine but lacking in teacher leadership experience. Here's what we learned from our first teaching experience and what we wish we'd known before we stepped into the classroom.

1. Find a mentor

Find a colleague who can be a mentor early on and learn from that person. Observe your mentor in and out of the classroom, with students and with colleagues, and then practice what you have observed, making it your own. Ask your mentor for advice and use it to improve your teaching.

2. You set the tone

We've all heard the phrase "attitudes are contagious." Get your students excited about coming to class and motivated to learn by maintaining an enthusiastic and positive attitude from the beginning of the course to the end. There will be times when you will feel frustrated—times when students are difficult. But showing these feelings in the classroom will not earn you the respect of students.

3. Have a vision for your class

Just as leaders have visions for their organizations, you need to have a vision for your class, and you need to regularly communicate it to students. Let students know what you hope to achieve and how. Sharing your road map for the course helps them understand and keeps you on track.

4. Communicate, communicate, communicate

Communication is the key to being a successful leader. According to Thomas Hoerr, author of *The Art of School Leadership*, a good leader communicates openly and honestly to build, maintain, and enhance relationships with students. Do everything you can to encourage open and honest communication in your classroom. Be responsive when students reach out to you. Be aware of your tone, whether you're speaking or writing to students. Even if your answers may not be the ones they want to hear, the manner in which you state them can make all the difference.

5. Be firm and fair even if it doesn't make everyone happy

Before making a decision, try to understand both sides of the issue, especially how it looks from the students' perspective. Explore the alternatives, considering both the benefits and drawbacks. Make sure your decision benefits the majority of those it will affect. Once you've decided, be firm and let your decision stand, even if it doesn't make everyone happy.

6. Take time to self-reflect

Take some time after each class to think about what happened. What worked? What didn't work? What would you change the next time? Don't be afraid of the mistakes you will make, but learn from them, capitalize on them, and turn them into successes. That's what effective leaders do.

7. Develop your own leadership habits . . . then realize that they might not work for every class

Effective leaders find habits that are successful for them, and they practice those habits. But even good habits aren't effective all the time. Sometimes what's worked well with one group of students won't work with another group. Be flexible and learn to modify these habits as the situation and your students change.

8. Not everyone will like you as a teacher

Even if you come prepared for class, maintain a positive attitude, develop good leadership habits, and are fair to your students, not everyone will like you as a teacher. Great leaders learn to look past the naysayers and focus on the fact that they are truly making a difference in some students' lives.

9. Learn to take the personal out of poor feedback

Evaluations filled out by your students are a great way to learn about your strengths and weaknesses in the classroom. They will contain positive and negative feedback. Try not to take the negative feedback personally and realize that these evaluations can be influenced by many factors. Maybe the student was having a bad day. However, if there are repeated suggestions for improvement in one area, make adjustments. Find your strengths and turn these into good leadership habits.

10. How to balance your life now that you are a teacher

A teacher's work seems never to be done. There's homework to correct, emails to answer, the next day's class to prepare, and grades to assign. Linda Lambert, author of Leadership Capacity for Lasting School Improvement (2003), writes, "It is essential to reserve time for ourselves. Without personal time, we lose focus and can overlook what's important in our rush to take care of what's urgent." Every great teacher leader needs to find a balance between work and home life.

Stepping into the classroom is an exciting and thrilling experience, but it can also be scary. We knew that we had the knowledge to teach our students, but we didn't realize that there was so much more to leading a class than just sharing our skills and knowledge. We needed to be leaders of learning, and that entailed lots of details we didn't anticipate.

Reprinted from *The Teaching Professor,* November 2012

Don't Waste the First Day

Kevin Brown

Despite the fact that numerous articles have been written on the importance of the first day, too many of us still use it to do little more than go over the syllabus and review basic guidelines for the course. This year I decided to try a different approach, and the results were much more dramatic than I expected. I taught real material on the first day. Despite that, there have been fewer questions about course policies, with some students actually referencing them without even a mention from me. Let me explain how I achieved these results.

On the first day (I used this approach in all my courses), I spent the majority of the time teaching content that related to the overall ideas of the course. Thus, in freshman composition, a course that focuses on experiential learning, I had the students go outside and experience a brief period of blindness. They took turns taping cotton balls over their eyes and leading each other around. We then analyzed the experience and talked about how one might craft a thesis to describe what happened. In a Western literature class, I introduced the major ideas of the Enlightenment and talked about how the interplay of reason and emotion would reoccur throughout the course.

Only after this exposure to course content did I give students a copy of the syllabus. Rather than going through it in detail, I told students that they were perfectly capable of reading it. I think we should start assuming that students ranging from developmental courses to upper-division major classes can read and understand a syllabus. Rather than treating the syllabus as something special, I decided to handle it as another reading assignment.

To prepare students for this reading assignment, I did a brief presentation (I used PowerPoint this year, which I almost never use) on the most important aspects of the syllabus: why students are taking the course, how to get in touch with me, our university's mission statement, academic support for those with disabilities, how to access the online readings, and the overall structure of the class. I limited the presentation to 10 minutes. I have even begun to wonder if I could skip handing out the syllabus altogether and simply have students print it off themselves and read it before coming to the first day of class.

On the second day, I had students pick up note cards as they arrived for class. I asked them to write on the card any questions they had about the syllabus. In one class of just over 30 students, I answered fewer than five questions, and it took less than five minutes. Even in my largest class, which had the most questions, I was still able to respond in less than 10 minutes. Thus, my presentation of the syllabus took 15 minutes, at best, as opposed to the 40 to 50 minutes it used to take.

I also used bonus questions taken from the syllabus on my reading quizzes. This makes it clear to students who have not read the syllabus that they are losing out on extra points. I have considered giving a quiz solely on the syllabus, as I have heard some professors do, but that seems a bit petty to me. I can see, though, how that approach reinforces the idea of treating the syllabus as class material, just like any other reading assignment.

In the past few weeks since the semester started, I have had more students reference policies from the syllabus than I usually have in an entire semester. Students know how many points I deduct for late papers, and two students in one class wanted to discuss our school's mission statement. They asked if I believed we are actually trying to live it out (we are a religious institution), something that has never happened in my eight years of teaching here.

Rather than wasting that all-important first day going over material students can read on their own, I recommend we begin by introducing students to ideas from the course. Almost all of us complain about running out of time by the end of the semester, but a better beginning can help us reclaim at least one day of it, if we use it wisely.

Reprinted from *The Teaching Professor,* November 2009

Skillful Teaching: Core Assumptions

Maryellen Weimer, PhD

Stephen Brookfield is out with a third edition of *The Skillful Teacher.* Only a handful of books on teaching make it past the first edition so to be out with a third says something about the caliber of this publication. He notes in the preface that the first edition appeared during year 20 of his teaching career. With this edition, he celebrates 45 years in the classroom. It seems more than appropriate to call the book a classic.

There's lots of new material in this third edition, certainly enough to warrant a purchase even if the first edition has a convenient place on the book shelf. But what hasn't changed are Brookfield's core assumptions about skillful teaching. They've stood the tests of time in his experience and that of many other skillful teachers. As Ruth Gotian notes on the endorsement page, "You are never too junior or too senior to apply these techniques," and that's why they merit reviewing here.

Skillful teaching is whatever helps students learn. "At first glance this seems a self-evident, even trite truism—a kind of pedagogic Hallmark greeting card. The problem is that an activity that helps one student learn can, to other students in the same class, be confusing and inhibiting. So taking this assumption seriously means our teaching becomes more, not less, complex." (pp. 15-16) This belief does add complexity to our teaching, but it can also free us from those instructional practices we think we should be doing. For Brookfield, the key question is whether what the teacher is doing is helping students learn? If it is, then that's what the teacher should be doing. Teaching is first, foremost, and fundamentally about learning. It has no reason to exist otherwise.

Skillful teachers adopt a critically reflective stance toward their practice. Critical reflection is what keeps teaching awake and alert. "It is mindful teaching practiced with the awareness that things are rarely what they seem." (p. 22) Teachers make assumptions all the time—about students, their learning, how well the class went—and that's not the problem. It's when we act on those assumptions without testing their accuracy. We assume the activity went well because students were smiling and looked engaged. Were they? More importantly, did that engagement promote learning? Did the activity deepen their understanding of the content? Did it lead them to new questions? Those questions are best answered, not by the teacher, but by students who participated in the activity, or by colleagues who observed it from a more objective position than the teacher who designed it, implemented it, and very much wants it to work. The activity itself should have been selected because it's been used elsewhere with positive results, or because the activity rests on premises that have been tested empirically. This kind of reflection is critical but not in the sense of endless fault-finding. It's a stance that re-energizes teaching and keeps teachers learning, growing, and anything but bored.

Teachers need a constant awareness of how students are experiencing their learning and perceiving teachers' actions. "We may exhibit an admirable command of content and possess a dazzling variety of pedagogic skills, but without knowing what's going on in our students' heads that knowledge may be presented and that skill may be exercised in a vacuum of misunderstanding." (p. 22) What Brookfield is describing here has nothing to do with student evaluations. It's descriptive, diagnostic input that enables teachers to understand the impact of their chosen policies, practices, assignments, and instructional methods on students' efforts to learn. It's not about what students want or what they like, but discovering what they need to help them learn. It's about the importance of teachers keeping their fingers on the pulse of the class and responding when that heartbeat changes.

College students of any age should be treated as adults. That's what students want. True enough, but often the typical 18- to 23-year-olds don't act like adults or they act like very immature adults. Could that be a reflection of how they've been treated or are being treated? Brookfield writes that students of all ages "don't like to be talked down to or bossed around for no reason, although they may be happy for the teacher to give them direction." (p. 24) Borrowing from Paulo Freire, they want teachers to be authoritative, not authoritarian. "They also want to be sure that whatever it is they are being asked to know or do is important and necessary to their personal, intellectual, or occupational development." (p. 24) College is about preparing people for life, and most of the time adults aren't treated like children in life.

Brookfield is such a fine writer. His books are warm, engaging, full of anecdotes, good ideas, and references to relevant research. Despite the fact that most academics are readers, we don't read a lot of books on teaching. We don't have time and we're hardly able to keep up with what's happening in our disciplines, but our teaching would be better if we did find time and used it to encounter explorations of skillful teaching like this one.

Reference
Brookfield, S. D. *The Skillful Teacher: On Technique, Trust, and Responsiveness in the Classroom.* 3rd Ed. San Francisco: Jossey-Bass, 2015.

Reprinted from *The Teaching Professor,* May 2015

Teaching as Storytelling

Dale Tracy

In a literature course in which students were struggling with poetry, I asked the class to talk about how they read. I prepared them with a series of questions. Do particular words or turns of phrase delight you? Do you skip long chunks of description to get more quickly to the next appearance of a character? Do you have trouble enjoying a text with characters you don't like? Do you more easily remember the plot summary or a certain scene from texts you've read? Students were happy to reflect on their reading tendencies and on my comments about how reading preferences shape understanding. The exercise demonstrated that learning has a plot. Hearing the range of strategies used by their classmates, students became aware that they were each living their own unique learning stories, stories that they are able to help shape.

Teaching is telling students a story that can intersect with these individual ones. Learning is a choose-your-own-adventure story in which students, guided by reflection on the learning process and course content, can recognize how their individual experiences become part of the story. The teaching story creates a through-line of the subject matter, the teacher, the students, and the broader learning contexts. When I teach, I narrate and shape this story in ways that help students recognize how much their self-reflection can be involved in learning. If I tell a story in which my students appear along with the subject matter, then they are invited to learn about themselves too.

By creating opportunities for students to approach learning not just as students but as people, learning may deepen from the understanding of course material to self-understanding. When learning is presented as a story, students are more likely to understand the material as relevant to their lives. I incorporate the person in teaching and learning, making flexible but structured space for students to consider their relationships to ideas, texts, and other people.

My goal is to enable students to risk approaching learning as people who might be affected by what they read and by what they create. Taking this risk depends on students' having confidence and finding a purpose in self-reflection.

I developed a strategy for facilitating such reflection while teaching a large second-year course. I had students write reflection paragraphs in response to prompts I gave them during lectures. This assignment grew out of those initial questions I asked students about how they read. I wanted them to reflect, to stop and think actively during lectures. Each prompt requires an individual response, and that helps create a relationship between each student and the subject matter. Since I did not formally grade these reflections—anyone who completed each reflection received a full participation mark—students were free to experiment and explore. Since I read and reported on the reflections, there was pressure to put effort into the assignment but not as much pressure to do it "right." Students had the time and reason to consider themselves, with less emphasis on what was expected of them and more emphasis on what they were honestly feeling and thinking in relation to the material.

Through reflection, students shape their learning identities. Through participation in discussion, they shape their learning communities. After the time for reflection and writing, I ask students to respond to the prompt verbally. This conversation allows students to share their ideas or questions with peers. In the following class, after I have read the reflections, I report back on common trends and make connections among the diverse ways of approaching the prompt. It also allows me to return to content the students struggled with, seeking new ways to explain it. I receive feedback on how the course is going from their responses as well.

A story is an engaging way to express ideas because it gives them meaning. Stories arrange diverse elements into meaningful combinations. In order to have students be active in conceptualizing their own learning, they need to know their own learning stories. If I teach material through the narrative of a learning community, I create the conditions for students to be aware of these stories.

Reprinted from *The Teaching Professor,* November 2014

Four Ways to Teach More Effectively

Maryellen Weimer, PhD

"No scientist wanting to remain at the leading edge of a field would use a research technique judged no longer as effective as an alternative. Shouldn't we apply the same standard to teaching?" (2151) Substitute the word "scholar" for "scientist," and it's a question that should be put to everyone who teaches. What's no longer deemed as effective is lecturing compared to the alternative of active learning. Many faculty members don't use much active learning even though many now acknowledge that they should. This article offers four ways to get started or to move forward in your use of active learning.

Design from Back to Front

Backward design as conceived by Wiggins and McTighe starts with course-level learning goals instead of content. You start with what you want students to know and be able to do at the end of the course. These large goals lead to learning objectives (i.e., what students will do to demonstrate that they've achieved the goals). Once you've got how the learning will be assessed, the content can be identified. Of course, students will need opportunities to practice and will need feedback to help them improve. Because backward design is so student-focused, it is difficult to implement without having students engaged in the hard, messy work of learning. It's a way to design courses that promote active learning.

For those with heavy teaching loads, course design (or redesign) sounds daunting, and while it is time consuming, the authors point out that you don't have to do a whole course all at once. You can start with one course goal and move back through objectives and assessment to content. The article also recommends some guides and other resources that can be helpful to faculty unfamiliar with backward design. In fact, at the end of this article there's a reference to a recent article that contains an excellent planning tool for incorporating backward design.

The point of this piece is well-taken. Most faculty don't think seriously about course design. More often they're focused on all that has to be covered in the course. Course design activities, most notably use of the backward design approach, can improve both teaching and learning.

Aim High, Beyond Just the Facts

Unfortunately, students get lots of practice memorizing facts. They become very good at it. What they aren't so good at is understanding why the facts are important or how they connect. Moreover, a focus on facts does not give students opportunities to think at higher levels.

What do teachers want students to know and be able to do five years after having taken the course? Of course, that will include some facts, but in most cases the facts will be supportive of the larger, more central concepts of the field. Isolated information bits don't easily coalesce into coherent understandings. Said another way, the content needs to stop being the end and start being the means faculty use to lead students to larger understandings and ways of thinking that typify how knowledge advances in a discipline.

Pose Messy Problems

Messy problems are those open-ended, rich, poorly structured, sometimes "wicked problems." They can't be answered directly. There isn't one right answer. And these are the kinds of problems most professionals face. Students can start learning how to handle these big real-life problems by practicing in our courses. But they are hard problems, and most students prefer quick and easy answers, so teachers must provide support and have realistic expectations. Students' abilities to deal with messy problems must be developed, but as their skills grow so does their level of engagement with each other and with course content.

Expect Students to Talk, Write, and Collaborate

"Through these activities, students can become aware of what they do not know or understand . . . which ideally prompts them to think more deeply or seek more information to clarify their understanding. The process of explaining requires students to integrate new and existing knowledge" (2153). Initially, these activities don't need to be complicated. The teacher can ask a question and students can talk with each other before the teacher solicits answers. Clickers can record first answers, which can then be discussed with others before they are answered a second time. Ideas and opinions can first be written down then shared and discussed. Students can learn from each other, and teachers can design activities that make that a more likely outcome.

The article concludes with straightforward and sanguine advice about learning to teach more effectively. It's good advice if you've just started moving in the direction of more active learning or if active learning is your preferred approach. All teachers can improve.

- Avoid reinventing the wheel. All sorts of good resources are available.
- Try one thing at a time. Start with something comfortable or tackle one of those parts of the class students routinely find difficult if you're more seasoned.
- Learn from colleagues. Watch them teach and let them watch you teach.
- Be transparent with students. After explaining what they need to do, ask them why you're having them do it that way. Don't assume what's obvious to you about your approach is equally apparent to them.

References

Dolan, E. L., and Collins, J. P. 2015. "We Must Teach More Effectively: Here Are Four Ways to Get Started." *Microbiology of the Cell* 26(June): 2151–2155.

Reynolds, H. L., and Kearns, K. D. 2017. "A Planning Tool for Incorporating Backward Design, Active Learning and Authentic Assessment in the College Classroom. *College Teaching* 65(1): 17–27.

Reprinted from *The Teaching Professor,* March 2017

Exploring What the Syllabus Communicates

Maryellen Weimer, PhD

The syllabus is often described as a road map to the course. But along with laying out the direction and details of the course, it also conveys messages about what the course will be like. These messages are not communicated explicitly but are more a function of the language and tone of the syllabus. A group of psychology faculty agreed, but they also wondered if the theoretical framework of the syllabus might influence students' perceptions of the course and its instructor.

To test that hypothesis, Richmond, Slattery, Mitchell, Morgan, and Becknell created two syllabi: one that represented learner-centered approaches to course design and one that represented teacher-centered approaches. They modified a rubric created by Cullen and Harris in a work published in *Assessment & Evaluation in Higher Education* and used it to guide construction of the two syllabi. The rubric identified learner- and teacher-centered factors in three areas: community (how accessible the teacher was), power and control (the focus of the syllabus with respect to policies), and evaluation and assessment (the relative emphasis on learning and grades). The learner-centered syllabus created for the study focused more on student learning, and the teacher-centered one focused more on the delivery of course content.

To ascertain whether each syllabus was correctly perceived as teacher- or learner-centered, they were blindly rated on 12 subfactors, derived from the three main factors, and both were correctly identified. Examples from each of the syllabi are included in the article.

These two syllabi were then given to 90 introductory psychology students, who received course credit for participating in the study. The students were given either the learner- or teacher-centered syllabus. They were told to read the syllabus, took a quiz on it, and then were asked to rate the instructor (who they were told wrote the syllabus) on 12 teacher behaviors taken from a Teacher Behavior Checklist (TBC), developed empirically, that listed the characteristic behaviors of master teachers (behaviors such as effective communication, preparation, enthusiasm, flexibility). They also rated the hypothetical teacher on another instrument that measures levels of teacher rapport with students.

The findings confirmed both of the authors' hypotheses. Students did perceive the instructor who wrote the learner-centered syllabus as having significantly higher master teacher behaviors than the instructor with the teacher-centered syllabus. They also rated the teacher with the learner-centered syllabus as having significantly higher rapport with students.

For instructors who worry about establishing connections with students in online courses, the results of this study are promising. They indicate that messages about who they are and what they hope will happen in the course can be conveyed by the course syllabus. It can be used to help set the tone for the course.

For instructors with face-to-face classes, there is an important caveat. The study setting was, in the words of the researchers, "highly controlled" and "artificial." In face-to-face courses, the syllabus is often delivered by the instructor who in most classes then talks about it at length. How the instructor's presence and discussion of the syllabus affects students' perceptions of it were not studied in this work. There are some instructors who now make the course syllabus available online before the class convenes so students may first review it without the instructor being present. We don't know at this time if their initial impressions are changed when they meet the instructor in person.

Whether the syllabus is first encountered with or without the instructor being present, work like this confirms the importance of this artifact of teaching. We've recognized its value as a road map for some time now. There are many articles and some books that delineate the various course details that can be included on the syllabus, often recommending a collection of them. What isn't as regularly recognized are these important "meta" messages that lurk between the lines of this course document. The syllabus subtly hints at what instructors believe about students, how much they care about learning, and whether the learning environment in the course will be open and inviting or closed and controlled. It's more than just a road map. The syllabus strongly suggests what the trip will be like.

Work like this should encourage us to look closely at our syllabi. What would students conclude about us and our course? It's an important part of how they are introduced to both.

Reference

Richmond, A. S., Slattery, J. M., Mitchell, N., Morgan, R. K., & Becknell, J. (2016). Can a learner-centered syllabus change students' perceptions of student-professor rapport and master teacher behaviors? *Scholarship of Teaching and Learning in Psychology, 2*(3), 1–10.

Reprinted from *The Teaching Professor,* December 2016

A Democratic Syllabus

Maryellen Weimer, PhD

It was a syllabus used in a small, upper-division political science seminar, which explains the name and the question of interest to the teacher of the course. "Can giving students more power over course content enhance their understanding of democratic authority and process?" (p. 167)

Three features of the course made the syllabus democratic, and they are features that could be incorporated into other courses. First, the instructor gave students some control over the seminar's discussion topics. The course began with two weeks' worth of teacher-selected introductory readings that addressed "the general idea and practice of democracy in America." (p. 168) Topics for the next five two-week-long sections were selected by student vote from a list of 22 subject areas.

Near the end of the semester, two weeks were devoted to student-led discussions. Each student selected the topic and readings and then led a half-period discussion of them. The teacher participated in these discussions as a student, limiting herself to one comment or question every 20 minutes.

Finally, students had some control over their two major assignments. In the first, they were given more than 100 websites important to democratic practice. They had to select five, visit those sites, and write short reflection papers about each experience. In the second assignment, they had to develop "a plan for expressing a public position or educating American citizens on an issue and then [execute] that plan, reflecting on the experience in writing." (p. 169) The instructor gave the students "wide latitude about when and how they completed their work, emphasizing that independent thought would be rewarded." (p. 169)

"Ultimately, my students and I deemed the democratic syllabus a great success in terms of both the classroom dynamics it created and the thinking about democratic politics that it encouraged," the instructor wrote. (p. 167) Student comments in the article offer insights on what made this a successful learning experience for them. They said that being able to select discussion topics increased their interest and investment in the course. "There wasn't a single class where I felt like we were talking about something that didn't matter," wrote one student. (p. 168) They also reported that deciding on discussion topics increased their sense of camaraderie. "All of us knew we were talking about these things because we wanted to."

Students also responded positively to the student-led discussions, as evidenced by one student writing that they "were among the best ones we had." (p. 168) The loose structure of the assignments generated some anxiety in the beginning, but once students got comfortable with the freedom, they used it to "think outside the box" and "do things I was really interested in."

It's a unique course design that blends content and learning processes in a way not possible in non-political science courses. But the syllabus design is worth considering in other courses, especially those upper-division, integrative seminar or capstone courses. It's also worth noting that despite giving students control over certain course decisions, the teacher still retained a significant amount of control. The teacher let students select discussion topics from a designated list, and once the topics were selected the teacher decided on the readings for each of those topics. The student-led discussions happened at the end of the course and in a two-week time frame, with teacher-led discussions up to that point in the course. The teacher proposed the basic assignment structure, with students free to fill in the details. As in democracies, there was a balance of power in this seminar.

The teacher does offer an important caveat: "Teaching a course with a democratic syllabus requires substantial work before and throughout the semester." (p. 170) There were course design challenges involved with creating the list of potential discussion topics. Whatever topics the student selected, discussion of that content had to result in a coherent course and one that met the course learning objectives. Once the students selected the topics, the teacher had to quickly assemble the readings that would be used to frame those discussions. The open-ended nature of assignments required consultation with students. This teacher estimates it took four times longer to run the course this way. The course also required more from the students. But a truly quality learning experience was the outcome. "More than a year later, I still hear from graduating seniors that this was the most important course they took in college." (pp. 167-8)

Reference

McWilliams, S. (2015). The democratic syllabus. *PS, Political Science and Politics, 48* (1), 167-170.

Reprinted from *The Teaching Professor,* April 2015

It Makes a Difference When Teachers Care

Maryellen Weimer, PhD

That's not a new finding, and it's something most instructors already know, but it's the size of the difference that's often underestimated. Two recent studies, both asking different research questions and using different methodologies, offer still more evidence that the relationship between teachers and students is an integral part of the learning experience.

"While we know a great deal about the kinds of faculty-student interactions students experience, the benefits of faculty-student interaction, and predictors of student-faculty interactions, we know little about what students themselves value in their interactions with faculty." (p. 126) And that's what prompted a faculty research team at North Carolina State University to undertake a qualitative analysis of a collection of feedback students had prepared for faculty. They used an interesting data pool. The institution sponsors a "Thank a Teacher" program, which encourages students to express appreciation and gratitude to professors. The research team used 157 comments written to professors by students who chose to use the program to offer their thanks.

The team used the data pool to answer two questions: (1) What do students value in their interactions with instructors? and (2) Do students express gratitude for interactions that align with National Survey of Student Engagement (NSSE) survey codes? They did find alignment with the NSSE codes, which is important since the NSSE measures of student-faculty interaction have guided much of the research in this area. They also found that this student cohort valued aspects of interactions with faculty that were beyond the scope of the NSSE measures.

Consistent with NSSE, these students valued being able to talk with faculty about what they needed to do to improve their performance in a class. They valued discussion about careers, including their academic career at college and career options after college. They valued being able to exchange ideas with professors and the constructive feedback some teachers provided. Beyond that, and even to a greater degree, these "students commended faculty for being understanding—especially in terms of devoting time to helping students out of class, caring, enthusiastic, and respectful of students." (p. 130)

This research team points out this about their data set: "Student responses suggest that, contrary to the perception that students value teachers who are merely 'easy' or 'fun,' students value high-quality interactions with faculty members." (p. 131) They value exactly the types of interactions that research has shown benefit them the most.

The second study explored the relationship between an instructor's self-rated commitment to students and student-rated satisfaction and commitment to the course. These researchers hypothesized that instructor commitment would be positively related to perceived instructor support. In other words, instructors committed to students would be seen by students as supportive teachers. This led to a second set of hypotheses. If students perceived instructor support, they would rate their satisfaction with the course higher, and this perceived support would mediate the relationship between instructor commitment and student satisfaction, as well as mediating the relationship between instructor and student commitment to the course.

They also used a unique research design. The student cohort consisted of 286 seniors, all graduating with degrees in management and all taking the same capstone course, but in one of five sections, each with a different instructor. So they gave the instructors a survey that measured their commitment to students, and they gave students a survey that measured how supportive they found the instructor, how satisfied they were with the course, and how committed they were to it as well. A rigorous empirical analysis produced data supportive of all three hypotheses.

"Our research found that perceived instructor support, driven by an instructor's commitment to teaching, influences both student satisfaction and student commitment. Students who believed that their instructor cared about their well-being and valued their contributions were more satisfied with their course and had higher commitment to the course." (p. 560)

Findings like these do advance our understanding of student-teacher interactions and relationships even though the findings are not surprising. These relationships have strong impacts on student learning experiences. But the faculty researchers in the first study that used the Thank a Teacher comments do make a point about something that they found surprising.

"These types of relationships with faculty are noteworthy enough to promote students to write a thank-you to their instructors, suggesting that these types of interactions are not nearly as commonplace as might be assumed." (p.131) In many of the comments included in the article, students are thanking faculty members for what ought to be considered part of the job—being there during office hours, helping when students didn't understand, and being respectful of students, for example.

Both studies recommend that faculty development activities focus less on teaching techniques—the how-to nuts and bolts—and more on the importance of these relationships and how faculty go about forming them and then conveying that commitment to students.

Reference
Grantham, A., Robinson, E. E., and Chapman, D., (2015). 'That truly meant a lot to me': A qualitative examination of meaningful faculty- student interactions. *College Teaching, 63* (3), 125-132.

Reprinted from *The Teaching Professor,* December 2015

Assignments: How Students Perceive Them

Maryellen Weimer, PhD

Assignments are one of those ever-present but not-often-thought-about aspects of teaching and learning. Nearly every course has them, and teachers grade them. The grade indicates how much the student learned by doing them. But is this learning something that students recognize? Too often students see assignments as work the teacher makes them do for a grade. How often do students see or experience assignments as learning opportunities?

We don't know much about students' perceptions of their assignments. Teachers don't often ask, and it's not an area that's been explored much empirically. Some descriptive work recently reported in *Teaching of Psychology* begins to uncover what students think about assignments and whether they are proud of their work and understand it as a learning experience.

In the first of two studies, the research team sought to determine if assignments engendered pride upon completion. Did students feel proud of their assignment work? The assumption, verified by related research, is that feelings of pride and accomplishment motivate effort, which should mean more learning. The researchers also wondered if students reported feeling proud of certain assignments. Could the assignment features that engendered this sense of accomplishment be identified?

To answer the question, researchers asked 113 undergraduates in four sections of an introductory psychology course to select the one of 19 assignments they completed that they were most proud of. This collection of assignments belonged to a category of work required in the course "Learning by Doing." They were described as "activities for you to observe and think like a psychologist" (p. 324). The assignments were graded as a set, and they counted for 20 percent of the overall course grade.

Students selected the task of responding to "what you consider to be your best assignment . . . the one you are most pleased with or most proud of" (p. 324) by explaining why they were pleased with it. Students chose from the 19 assignments, and statistical analysis revealed that "yes, academic assignments can be distinguished on the basis of the feeling of pride they are associated with" (p. 324).

The assignments themselves were content-specific and, therefore, not as interesting to those outside the field as the reasons students gave for selecting them. Three themes emerged, starting with *effort*. If students worked hard on the assignments, they felt that sense of pride. Second, the assignment engendered pride if it had *self-relevance*. This theme is broadly defined. Sometimes the relevance was a function of students' connecting with the field as an area of intended study. In other cases, it was that the assignment had personal relevance. For example, the assignment most often chosen as the one students felt proud of involved a self-assessment that explored personality and career choice. The final theme involved *recognition by others*, which in this case consisted of positive feedback from the teacher.

In the second study, the researchers asked "whether variation in pride associated with the assignments were correlated with student judgments that the assignment was a useful teaching tool" (p. 326). Said more directly, they asked whether students thought they had learned something by doing the assignment. The methods and procedure were the same, but in the second study a different student cohort and smaller collection of assignments were used. At the end of the semester, students were asked to select the assignment they learned the most from and the assignment they were most proud of. Here as well, they were asked to give reasons for their choices.

Three themes emerged here as reasons for selecting the assignments; the *time and effort* and *self-relevance* themes were present in this data set along with a new third theme, *helped me understand the course material*. For the assignment students said they learned the most from, 42 percent said the reason was that it helped them understand the course material. However, with the assignment they were most proud of, only 2 percent said the reason was because the assignment helped them understand course material. In other words, if the assignment required time and effort, the student got involved in doing the assignment, which caused pride far more regularly than what they learned from doing the assignment.

The authors of the study note, "The findings of this study suggest that in planning a course it might be wise for instructors to balance assignments that simply and clearly elucidate course material with those that demand the time and effort (student complaints not withstanding) to create a prideful experience" (p. 327).

Reference
Pines, H. A., Larkin, J. E, and Murrary, M. P. (2016). Dual outcomes of psychology assignments: Perceived learning and feelings of prideful accomplishment. *Teaching of Psychology, 43*(4), 323–328.

Reprinted from *The Teaching Professor,* November 2016

Writing Good Assignment Descriptions

Maryellen Weimer, PhD

Concern about the quality of student writing is ongoing and not without justification. Faculty are addressing the problem with more writing assignments and a concerted faculty effort to improve student writing across the curriculum. Authors Allison Rank and Heather Pool, who during their graduate work directed a political science writing center, laud these faculty efforts but point out that faculty are not looking carefully at their writing in the assignment descriptions they give students. "We argue that the intent, structure, and working of a prompt all help promote or impede student writing." (p. 675) In this very detailed article, they offer advice and suggestions on writing better assignment prompts. The article's many examples are drawn from political science, but the advice and suggestions offered are broadly applicable.

The authors aspire to give teachers guidance "about how to actually write a clear and doable writing assignment, pitched at the right level to achieve specific aims." (p. 676) They start with an updated version of the Bloom taxonomy, to which they add further modifications. Writing assignments can be designed to achieve five cognitive objectives, listed from low to high, as in the Bloom hierarchy: 1) to summarize, which demonstrates a grasp of previously presented material; 2) to relate, which develops connections among concepts, events, and actors; 3) to analyze, which deconstructs arguments using logic and disciplinary standards; 4) to evaluate, which involves assessing claims according to disciplinary standards; and 5) to create, which involves generating content ranging from research questions to policy proposals. (p. 677)

They recommend appropriate terms for prompts at each of these levels and identify the benefits to students and instructors of each objective in a helpful table on page 677. Assignment terms should be used precisely. For example, the terms "describe" and "discuss" mean different things. Describe means "to give a detailed account," and discuss means to "offer a considered and balanced review that includes a range of arguments, factors or hypotheses." (p. 676) To ask students to do both in a single question can lead to confused and muddled responses.

They make the same point about an assignment that contains multiple questions. "Instructors often use a host of questions that seem to be clear and in order, but students frequently respond with paralysis." (p. 678) Beginning writers may struggle to identify the central and supporting questions. They respond with papers that are not structured around a clear thesis statement. Authors Rank and Pool recommend identifying primary and secondary questions for beginning writers and encouraging more advanced writers to consider the relationships between questions before they start writing. Differentiating between multiple questions as they write assignment prompts can also help instructors see whether the goals of the assignment align with course objectives.

The article also contains a discussion of each of the five writing assignment cognitive objectives, which are summarized briefly below:

Summarize: "These prompts (define, summarize, describe, identify) require [students], in their own words, to communicate information covered in lectures, readings, or prior classes." (p. 678) The authors recommend using these prompts in low-stakes, free-writing assignments when the instructor needs feedback on the levels of student understanding. This writing can also be used in class to promote discussion.

Relate: "Asking students to *relate* two distinct analyses works best when they have been prepared by thinking about theories or events in conceptually related ways that are held together by major ideas or questions." (p. 678)

Analyze: Writing assignments here involve disciplinary standards. Students are being asked to critically engage with course material by applying disciplinary rules for making and supporting arguments, for example. Students might be asked to "consider an argument or concept in a way that uncovers the assumptions and interrelationships of the issue." (p. 679) These are the kinds of writing assignments that develop students' abilities to critically analyze

Evaluate: Prompts that ask students to evaluate benefit them in three ways: 1) they are exposed to the standards of evidence-based inquiry, 2) they are being asked to consider the implications of theories being discussed in the course, and 3) they do not have to simply accept conclusions offered by authorities but are being challenged to evaluate those conclusions.

Create: Here students do writing assignments in which they use the knowledge and skills gained in the course to create new knowledge. At the high end of the Bloom taxonomy these are the most challenging writing assignments and the ones that require significant preparation before they can be successfully completed.

Beyond these five cognitive objectives for writing assignments, the authors make a strong case for writing assignments that ask students to reflect on their learning. "We encourage instructors who ask students to write multiple papers to also ask them to reflect on how the feedback on their first paper influenced their approach to the second." (p. 680)

The authors rightly observe that the literature is full of descriptions of different kinds of writing assignments, different ways those assignments can be integrated in non-writing courses, and different approaches to assessing writing, but there is precious little advice "about *how* we ask students to write." (p. 680) This very well-written article does an excellent job of filling that gap.

Reference

Rank, A., and Pool, H. (2014). Writing better writing assignments. *PS, Political Science and Politics, 47* (3), 675-681.

Reprinted from *The Teaching Professor,* January 2015

Creating Effective Handouts

Maryellen Weimer, PhD

For most of us, handouts are a staple of instructional life, but as Teresa Sakraida and Peter Draus (reference below) point out, their "development is often a trial-and-error process." (p. 326) Like so many other aspects of instruction, we take the construction of handouts for granted, disregarding that their various uses implicate their design. Intuition guides the creation of most handouts.

The article referenced identifies a range of purposes for handouts. They can function as advance organizers, previewing and preparing students for what's to come. They can introduce activities, describe the task, offer advice on process, and identify outcomes. They can expedite progress through material by providing students with drawings, graphs, or other data that take excessive time to replicate by hand. They can offer a break during a lecture, allowing students to read instead of listen. They can serve as study guides, containing summaries and highlights of key points covered in class or in the text. They can convey other messages, such as an instructor's interest in the material, a humorous anecdote, or good advice on successful study strategies.

Instructors used to duplicate handouts and distribute them in class—today technology makes it easy and convenient to provide materials on a course website, along with links to other related and relevant sources.

The design features of successful handouts are more than just a matter of advice—they have been studied and are recommended based on empirical analyses of features known to expedite the learning process. Among the most important design features is the need to **keep the handout simple**, especially when it's being used as a presentation aid. Don't include a lot of unnecessary detail; keep the focus on a single topic.

It is also important to **consider the visual impact of the handout**. In part this relates to its functionality. If students are to take notes on the actual handout, make sure that there's enough space to do so. It's easy to check this by looking at notes that students have previously written on the handout. Visual impact also involves how information on the handout is configured. Is white space being used to organize and highlight the information? Lists are frequently easier to follow than points buried in a paragraph. Technology makes it easy to manipulate many more design elements. Font size and style can be changed. Color can be incorporated. In fact, technology makes so much easily possible that the visual details can become distracting. Rather than supporting the content, they can become more memorable than the content, or worse yet, they can detract from what's most important.

Finally, do not underestimate the importance of **using handouts that look professional**. If the message conveyed to students is that spelling counts, then the teacher's spelling ought to be exemplary. Handouts should be carefully proofread. If material from other sources is used, it should be properly referenced. If material is secured by copyright, that too should be acknowledged. As information changes, content on the handout should be kept current through regular updates.

None of this advice is new or unknown, but it behooves us all to sit down every once in a while and carefully consider the collection of handouts used in a course. Better yet, have students pull out the ones they have tucked into their notebooks or list the ones they remember using online; then give them the opportunity to provide some constructive feedback. It's not that most handouts are bad; it's that most handouts could be made better.

Reference

Sakraida, T. J., & Draus, P. J. (2005). Quality handout development and use. *Journal of Nursing Education*, 44(7), 326–329.

Reprinted from *The Teaching Professor*, October 2005

Successful Classroom Management

Maryellen Weimer, PhD

Managing students who are disruptive, those who lack motivation and appear as though they would rather be any place than in the classroom, is easier when faculty take the right stance. Anything is possible when faculty have faith in the students they teach. Learning starts with a dedicated teacher interested in meeting the challenge of how to present content in a way that successfully navigates the barriers students erect.

Believing in students is the right stance, but it doesn't prevent students from coming to class unprepared, handing in assignments late, asking for exceptions, and talking in class. The principles of Motivational Enhancement Therapy, originally developed by W.R. Miller and S. Rollnick to help college professionals engage students with drinking problems, offer strategies that faculty can use with disruptive students in class. Each of the four principles described below has the professor acknowledging the problem and then working with the student to develop a plan to correct the problem. It's an approach built on collaboration.

Express empathy: The professor communicates with the students from a position of power, but the professor still respects the student and practices active listening. Despite the power associated with being the professor, the teacher recognizes that the behavior that needs to be changed can be changed only by the student.

Develop discrepancy: Students are motivated to change when they perceive a discrepancy between where they are and where they want to be. The professor can make students aware of this discrepancy. "You want an A in this course and yet you are regularly losing points by not being in class to take the quizzes." "You want to be a successful manager and yet you fall asleep whenever you lose interest. What's going to happen when the staff meetings you're required to attend get boring?"

Avoid argumentation: Arguing with students only makes them more resistant. It is highly unlikely that the professor is going to persuade a student (whether that student needs to come to class or get work done on time). A more indirect approach may be better. "When you miss class, you are wasting money. You pay for each class and get nothing when you aren't there."

Roll with resistance: Don't meet it head on. Invite the student to think about the problem differently. Rather than imposing a solution, see if the student might not be able to generate one. "You missed the assignment. What's a fair consequence for that?"

College professors aren't law enforcement officers. They aren't expected to be entertainers or hand-holders. They do have the responsibility to create a classroom setting that engages students and fosters relationships based on mutual respect. Students should not IM in class or arrive late or hungover any more than professors should show up the minute class begins, lecture, and leave promptly when it's over. Learning occurs when both work together, treading softly on differences and celebrating strengths.

Reprinted from *The Teaching Professor,* October 2008

Taking Risks in Your Teaching

Maryellen Weimer, PhD

Often in workshops when I'm speaking about the process of implementing change—deciding what to change and how to change it or considering whether to add a new instructional strategy—the question of risk lurks in the choices being considered. When attending a workshop or program that offers a range of instructional possibilities, teachers typically respond to some favorably. I see it—they write down the idea, nod, or maybe ask a follow-up question to be sure they understand the details. Not all the ideas presented get this favorable response. Occasionally, the response is overtly negative. But more often there is no response. The idea doesn't resonate.

When I ask participants to look over their notes (I love teaching faculty because they do take notes) and share what criteria they used to select the new ideas they're considering implementing, the responses are pretty non-specific: "I liked it." "It's something I think I can do." "I can use it when I'm teaching X." I think they are really saying, "This approach fits comfortably with who I am and how I teach." We first gravitate toward instructional changes that mesh with current practices and the content we teach. We choose them because we can see ourselves doing them.

And I think that's a legitimate criterion, especially for less-experienced teachers. You need to construct a solid base of instructional practices that work for you, given your content and the students you teach. But when you're an experienced teacher, sometimes you want to move beyond the comfortable, easy to implement, I-know-I-can-make-it-work alternatives. Instructional risk-taking has merit. Anytime we do things outside our comfort zone, we do so with a heightened sense of awareness, greater mental acuity, and, yes, more fear. The possibility of failure is a reality when we're doing something that we haven't done before. But the possibility for new insights and new levels of understanding is also a reality.

Any instructional practice that is new to you, such as group testing, giving students a role in creating a classroom policy, or getting students involved in assessment, is not just a new activity that requires attention to a new set of implementation details; it's a practice that shines light on fundamental beliefs about teaching and learning. It raises questions, challenges what we believe, and enables us to consider how aspects of teaching and learning look when viewed from a different perspective. Maybe our beliefs can't change, or maybe the practice doesn't fit with a particular educational philosophy, but isn't it better to have at least considered it or tried so we can say with authority that it's at odds with what we believe?

What worries me is that those new strategies that we don't write down or consider are initially rejected, not because they don't fit with our educational philosophies, but because they feel risky. We haven't done them and can't see ourselves doing them, or we hide behind our suppositions that students won't like the new approach. ("I don't use group work because students tell me they hate it.")

Are some instructional approaches just too risky? Can teachers take on something they really shouldn't be trying? Of course. I do worry that teachers sometimes try to implement too many changes at once; although, as my good colleague Larry Spence regularly points out, some teachers need to throw out the syllabus and reconstruct the course from the ground up. There are times and circumstances that merit much change. There are also times that merit making a change that feels risky. Teachers committed to career-long growth and development need every now and then to throw caution to the wind and sail into class with an instructional approach that takes them into new, uncharted waters. Chances are the prevailing winds will lead them and their students to a place of rich learning.

Reprinted from *The Teaching Professor,* March 2014

PART 2

•

Student Learning

Reaching Students

Maryellen Weimer, PhD

Occasionally I read old issues of *The Teaching Professor* newsletter, usually looking for something I vaguely remember. Sometimes I find it and other times I don't, but pretty much always I stumble across something that I've completely forgotten that I wish I'd remembered. Case in point: an insightful piece offering a series of lessons learned after the first five years of teaching (it's in the February 2009 issue). I love the piece for its honesty. Some of the most important lessons about teaching are those most of us have had to learn the hard way.

Author Graham Broad writes: "At some point in the past year I decided that my initial belief that I could 'reach' *all* students, and that *all* teaching problems could be resolved through correct pedagogy, wasn't optimism, it was egotism. Some students, I have come to understand, just aren't that into me."

Reaching students means connecting with them, and even the seasoned among us sometimes forget just how strongly students do identify with us as persons. If you need a reminder, take a look at the piece in this issue that reports on the results of a qualitative analysis of comments on the Rate My Professor site. We could attribute the value students place on having "nice" professors to immaturity. We could point out that our job descriptions don't stipulate that students have to like us. And we would be correct. However,

if students don't feel some sort of rapport with the teacher, that gets in the way of learning, especially when students aren't intrinsically motivated by our content.

That said, Broad's insight reveals another important point about connecting with students. It makes sense, and maybe we even have a professional responsibility to try to reach all students, but we are destined to fail with some, and it's egotistical to imagine otherwise. Students and teachers are all unique human beings. We wear our individuality in different ways. Some of those ways are meaningful to some students and not to others. Part of the maturity we need includes an acceptance of the fact that who we are and how we teach may be genuine and authentic, but that we will still not connect with certain students. Now, if we regularly don't connect with significant numbers of students, that is an issue, but not for now.

We don't always think about how diverse the college experience is for students. They take courses with diverse content, all (or most) taught by different teachers. Chances are good that students will connect with a teacher, maybe even several. It doesn't take a connection with every teacher to make a potent educational experience. How many of us have those favorite stories of that one encounter with a teacher that changed the direction of our lives? So, when we've got one (or several) of those students who don't respond to our attempts to connect, we don't take it personally, we don't give up with that student, and we keep our fingers crossed that in some other course with some other professor that student will make one of those connections that shifts their educational experience into higher gear.

Reprinted from *The Teaching Professor,* April 2015

How Can I Communicate to Motivate and Engage my Students?

Jennifer Waldeck, PhD

I have to admit, when I first started talking about teaching to audiences that represented different disciplines, I learned that a lot of college professors are stuck on their content. They believe that it, along with the pedagogy that they use for presenting, is what causes learning to occur. Now it's true that credible, effective teachers are, first and foremost, subject matter experts. Years of education and experience have helped us build this knowledge base that we use as the foundation for our teaching, then we work hard at developing unique, innovative, in-class pedagogy and assignments for our students.

But why, then, despite our expertise and effort, do we still struggle to get our students engaged, motivated, and understanding what we want for them as students? Years of research suggests that the secret sauce, so to speak, is communication. More specifically, the way a teacher communicates plays a powerful role as the source of all kinds of messages in and around the college classroom.

In fact, research reveals that no other source is as powerful than the teacher on student outcomes like motivation, compliance, enjoyment of the class, student intentions of what they plan to do with what they learn, and their learning outcomes—things like recall, understanding, analysis, synthesis, and so on. It's not your content, it's not your textbook, it's not what fancy technologies you select, and it's not even primarily the characteristics of your students, even though all of these things matter to an extent.

Scientifically speaking, what causes learning is a complex interaction of factors, the most important of which are the instructor's communication skills and choices. These operate to get students in a state of what I call "readiness to learn."

That same research reveals that, in order to accomplish these positive things, we need to be very careful in our interactions with students. Their perceptions of us matter greatly. They notice our missteps that sometimes we aren't even aware of. They are very sensitive to anything we say or do that they might experience as negative or antisocial, and this effects their capacity for learning.

But sometimes we must deliver negative feedback or talk about topics that our students think of as unpopular or unpleasant. So, the question becomes, how do we do all of that without coming across as a negative, overbearing, domineering, controlling teacher? The answers are critical to our success, because when students perceive us in these negative ways, their achievement, along with our teacher ratings, almost always suffer.

The answer to the question lies in a concept that was first studied by the respected UCLA psychologist Albert Mehrabian in the 1960s and '70s. It was first applied to the study of education by communication researchers in the late '70s. It's known as "immediacy." "Immediacy" refers to communicators' perceptions of physical and psychological closeness with one another.

Immediacy is connected to all kinds of desirable things, in all different types of communication settings, not just teaching. Work, families, dating relationships, marriages, healthcare situations, and so on. Since the early 1980s, research on teachers' habits, though, that result in students' perceptions of immediacy has been very, very clear. We know that when students perceive teachers to be consistently and authentically immediate, the list of great things that happen is very long.

First, they tend to view us as more likable than their less-immediate teachers. And, by extension, they're led to like the content of our courses. When a teacher is liked, respected, and admired by students, research is very clear—those students learn more than they would enrolled in a class with a teacher they don't like, don't respect, or don't admire. Students enrolled in classes with highly immediate teachers are more cooperative and willing to do the things we ask them to do. They view immediate teachers as credible, competent, trustworthy, caring, and responsive experts.

When we're immediate, our students are less anxious and stressed about their performance, even in courses that are famous for creating a lot of anxiety, like statistics, public speaking, or math. When we're immediate, our students experience greater motivation. They use their communication devices, like phones and laptops, for social reasons during class a lot less often.

When students experience us as immediate and approachable, they often experience feelings of being mentored, rather than just taught. They feel like they're getting a personalized educational experience, and not like a number or just a body in a seat. Immediate teachers also are very successful at empowering students in the learning experience to take a greater role, rather than a passive one, in their learning. They perceive greater understanding of material on any given day, regardless of other factors, when we're immediate, such as whether they read the book or did the homework.

When teachers are immediate, students are more likely to persist in college rather than drop out. They interpret our feedback more constructively and objectively rather than personally and defensively. They're less likely to be uncivilized, resistant, and disruptive in how they talk with us.

When we're truly immediate, our students view us as assertive—but not aggressive. They then tend to respect our policies and what we ask of them. Students enrolled in courses with immediate teachers learn more, they perform better on tests, they get better grades, and they even report feelings of more mastery and achievement.

When we're immediate, we get higher teacher ratings, not only from our students, but from our supervisors and peers who evaluate us. We have greater power to be persuasive and influential over our students and what they learn when we're immediate. I warned you the list was long, but no other teacher-communication behavior is more important to student learning than immediacy.

Immediacy works based on a simple principle that Mehrabian studied—that people are drawn toward that which they like or prefer, and then they move away from, or avoid, the things that they don't like or prefer. Since the research is very clear on just how much of a role we as teachers play in student learning, it stands to reason that we want our students to approach us and what we're trying to do in and around our classes.

I use that phrase "in and around our classes" a lot, because I don't believe that the need for masterful communication is limited to our formal class time with students. If we want students to visit us in our offices—and the research tells us that that can be a very valuable experience—we have to be capable, likable, approachable communicators there, too. This also applies to the campus coffee shop, before and after class, in the hallways, anywhere we run into students.

Now if you're one of those teachers who thinks, you know, "I'm busy. I'd rather students not approach me too much," I really want to encourage you to rethink that philosophy. It's only through interpersonal encounters that students reduce their misunderstanding, their anxiety about learning and performance, and develop positive attitudes about what we're teaching. It's through the relationships that they form with us that they become motivated and get the information that's necessary for their learning. The old spray-and-pray approach—that is, spray them with information in class and then just pray that they get it—is really a completely ineffective way to teach.

So how do we become more immediate teachers? Well, it starts with developing a repertoire of both verbal and nonverbal communication skills. First, what we say can cause our students to feel closer or more distant to us. We can increase immediacy and reduce distance from our students by developing habits that show our openness. And one of the most important things that you can do is say things to your students that encourage them to communicate with you.

Behave in ways and say things that suggest your warmth and that you care about your students. Say things that illustrate that you can see your student's perspective, even if ultimately you do want to move them around and influence them to see your perspective. Here are some things to try, in order to be more verbally immediate.

Use terms like "we" and "us" to refer to your class, instead of "you." Allow for some small talk and out-of-class conversations with students. I like to come in a few minutes early, whenever it's possible, and I'm very open to students who want to talk. And I like to be the last one out of the classroom, in case somebody needs to speak to me then.

Try engaging in a little bit of self-disclosure. Of course, it has to be appropriate—not too much, and it shouldn't go on too long. The topic shouldn't be too personal, but it can't hurt to talk about your summer vacation or what you did over the weekend, and encourage students to do the same. Even simple questions like "How was your weekend?" or "Do you have any plans for break?" are going to get you some great return on a very small communication investment.

Another way to be immediate is to give students feedback. Even respond to their comments and answers in class. Simple things like "Hey, that's really interesting, thanks," can be very effective.

Ask students how they feel about things going on in class. Know your students' first names. Learn them very quickly in the semester and use them. When I train new teachers, I tell them that this is actually the most important thing that they need to do, the first week of class. Even in large classes, learn some of the names, and maybe try to come up with a system, like a seating chart, that will let you use names when you want to talk to students or call on those that raise their hand.

These verbal-immediacy strategies are important when we deal with students, but the research indicates that nonverbally immediate communication may have an even greater impact on students and their learning. Nonverbal immediacy behaviors are some of the most valuable things in your teaching tool kit. So, what can you do to be a nonverbally immediate teacher?

First, gesture when you're talking to the class. Use your hands and your arms to emphasize important points. Use vocal variety when talking to your class. Some people don't think of the use of the voice as nonverbal, but it is, technically speaking. So, don't be a monotone teacher.

Look at the class while talking to them. Make sure that you make eye contact and briefly sustain it with everyone in the room at some point during the class. In large lectures where it's not possible to make eye contact with everyone, create zones in your mind, and make sure that you hit each zone, since every student isn't possible.

Smile at the class. Make sure that you have a friendly facial expression, that you're animated, and that you smile whenever you can. Make sure your posture is relaxed. Don't be too stiff and formal. When students approach you to talk, stand within what we call "personal distance," which is about one to four feet. Be mindful, all the time, the worst thing you can do is back up. So just be careful that you don't do that.

Move around the classroom when you teach. Make use of all your available space. And make sure you do it in large lectures, too. I even go and stand at the very back of the room, from time to time. This even gives me a chance to see what's going on on students' laptops, and so on.

Avoid being too dependent on your notes when you teach. That interrupts eye contact and this immediacy that we're really aiming for. Never turn your back to students for more than a second or so. And avoid that habit of talking to the screen or the board. Talk to your students.

Remove barriers between yourself and your students. Never stand behind the podium for any length of time to teach. And when students come to your office, if you have the space, try to come out from behind your big desk to work with them.

The way you dress is a powerful nonverbal-immediacy behavior. Be professional but more casual. Research indicates that when teachers dress too formally, students feel that they're competent, but maybe not very caring or receptive. And, as a result, students don't see us as approachable.

So, I suggest that, to get the ball rolling when it comes to credibility—and especially for new teachers—start out by dressing more professionally for the first class meeting or two, and then ease up, getting more casual throughout the semester. There is also some research that suggests your style matters. Students assign more credibility to teachers whose clothes are up to date. You don't need to be trendy, just make sure you're in this decade.

Hygiene matters, too. Remember, your appearance is the first thing that students sense about you, and it's human nature to draw conclusions, both accurate and inaccurate, based on first impressions. Remember that the good news is you can exercise control over your first impression by being a strategic, immediate communicator.

I coach a lot of new instructors, and a lot of them are resistant to some of these things that I'm recommending. They express some concern that these suggestions will undermine their authority, or that developing communicative relationships with students might be a risky thing to do.

They believe that interacting beyond the simple purposes of transmitting information or answering content questions will lead to too much informality, a lack of discipline or rigor. They worry that they won't be able to uphold the boundaries of their policies if they really start communicating with their students.

I've heard things like "Well, I teach in a law school. We aren't really friendly with our students." In response, I'll say right away that you really need to look at immediacy as something critical, no matter what you teach. It's a personality requirement for what we do. But, with that said, when you think back on the things I've suggested, you are probably more comfortable with some than others. Some of them might be highly unusual for your field or not the norm in your department.

So, in terms of your own comfort zone, it's important to practice those behaviors with your students that you feel comfortable with. It has to be authentic for it to work. This is not about faking it. Your students will know if these behaviors don't reflect your real feelings.

For those of you who just believe that some of these things are not appropriate or who work in disciplines where immediacy is not the norm, don't be defensive. Don't try to rationalize or insist that the way you do things is better. Entertain the notion that change might bring you positive results, that there might not be a sound reason, other than tradition, for the norms of formality and distance and authority.

I'm not suggesting that teachers and students are on the same level, that they should be friends or act like peers. I'm just asking you to consider the fact that when we're immediate, students aren't so intimidated by us. They're more likely to ask questions and engage with us. And they're more comfortable in our classes.

Immediate teachers are also versatile communicators. They know when to be friendly, warm, and approachable, and they know when immediacy is not the message that they want to send. For immediate teachers, it's also easy to make requests, disagree, express their own rights, rules, and policies, create boundaries, and so on.

The reality of most teaching professors is that they are brilliant experts at what they teach, but not necessarily how to teach or how to communicate with students. Unfortunately, most teachers have little formal education in the field of communication, beyond maybe a public-speaking class. Speaking skills are very helpful, but they're just a small portion of the communication skills that are important for teachers.

Now you have a new set of skills that are critical to your teaching effectiveness. You're probably already using a number of them, without even realizing how important they are. So, it's time to view them in a new light, use more of them, and do it consistently.

Adapted from the Magna 20-Minute Mentor program "How Can I Communicate to Motivate and Engage my Students?"

What Students Understand Isn't Always What the Professor Means

John A. Dern

For most of my 19 years as a teacher, I retained rather rigid control over assigning grades in my classes. My students did not participate in the process until recently. A couple of summers ago, I read a book on learner-centered teaching, and it, along with some urging from my program, persuaded me to try releasing a modicum of that control. To that end, I developed an "Attendance and Participation Self-Evaluation Form."

This optional end-of-semester self-evaluation asks students to do a basic analysis of their attendance and participation in regard to specific course requirements. For instance, in addition to asking students whether or not they participated in class discussions or exceeded the permitted number of absences for the semester, the form inquires about whether students brought texts to class with them, and completed required blog or discussion board assignments. In addition, the form leaves space for students to comment on their performance and argue for the grade they propose. I award one grade for a combination of attendance and participation.

I used this form during the 2009-10 academic year, and more than 50 percent of my students proposed their own non-binding grades for the attendance/participation portion of their final grades. I was generally pleased with the rate of response, and I felt some measure of satisfaction at having given students the opportunity to play even a small role in the assessment process. However, an analysis of the fall semester forms revealed that some students did not interpret *participation* the way I do.

After considering the feedback provided by 43 students during the fall semester, I raised 16 percent of the proposed attendance/participation

grades, maintained 37 percent, and lowered 47 percent. Some of the proposed grades were lowered because students had not completed other work,
such as blog assignments. However, some of the students had proposed
grades based on a different interpretation of "participation" than my own.
For instance, about 21 percent of students interpreted listening or being
attentive as "participation." Indeed, one student observed that she "always
took notes and paid attention to the lecture and discussion."

In my fall syllabi, I had written that the attendance/participation grade
was a combination grade, and I went on to explain that "exuberant participation" did not guarantee an "A" if "excessive absences" were also part of
the record. I assumed that the phrase "exuberant participation" and, indeed,
the word "participation" itself, were self-explanatory and denoted *vocal*
participation. I also assumed that the simple differentiation between the
two facets of the grade—"attendance" and "participation"—implied
that denotation.

I decided I would further clarify "participation" in my spring semester
syllabi in the hope of preventing further misunderstanding. Specifically, I
noted, "The instructor does not consider *attentiveness* to be participation.
Rather, participation includes vocally engaging the instructor and the class
during discussions, and contributing to group work." The student responses
from the spring semester suggest that this explanation helped. During that
semester, based on self-evaluations received from 39 students, I raised 15
percent of their proposed grades, maintained 49 percent, and lowered 36
percent. (Again, I lowered some grades because of missing work.) For this
semester, a greater percentage of students and I agreed on their participation
grades. More to the point, the forms revealed a decline in the number of
students (8 percent) who specifically associated listening or attentiveness
with participation. (In fairness, another 8 percent suggested that they had
participated by taking notes, which could be construed as a variation on the
"listening" argument.)

This article is not about whether a teacher should or should not grade
"participation," nor is it about the virtues of student self-assessment per se.
The message of this article is that student interpretations of what constitutes
fulfillment of a requirement like "participation" can differ from teacher
interpretations even when a teacher assumes the requirement is self-explanatory. To avoid miscommunication, teachers need to make themselves aware
of their own assumptions and work to clarify their expectations for students.

Reprinted from *The Teaching Professor,* November 2010

Questions: Why Do They Matter?

Patty Kohler-Evans

In his *Letters to a Young Poet*, Rainer Maria Rilke urged the younger correspondent to learn to love questions, even those that were unanswered. This admonition has stuck with me for several decades, especially in times when I am seeking answers to seemingly tough questions. In thinking about actually loving questions, I contemplated my own relationship with them, and I realized that asking questions is one of a teacher's most essential responsibilities. The act of posing a query is one of the characteristics that actually sets this profession apart. Reflecting on this epiphany, I wondered if and how exactly I pose evocative and powerful questions. I decided that there are several opportunities to place a well-developed inquiry, and I wanted to share those. The "Who are you?" questions are ones we direct to ourselves; the "What are you thinking?" questions are ones we need to ask our students; and the "So what?" questions are for students to ask themselves—with a little prompting from us, naturally.

The most important questions: Who are you?

So much of teaching centers around the relationships we develop with our students. We start with our content; it's our reason for being. We teach because we want to grow the next cadre of scientists, teachers, lawyers, engineers, and doctors. What we teach is incredibly critical, but I sometimes wonder if we are focused enough on *who* we teach. Here are a few questions I have thought about in my own contemplation of students and my relationships with them: To what degree do we see our students as unique individuals? How do we invest time in seeking to know them and understand a bit about their lives, beliefs, and aspirations? How do we ask, "Who are you?" How important is asking to our profession? How important is it to our students? How do we convey that we are invested in them as the next generation of torchbearers for our work? How do we witness their struggles without fixing their problems? How do we get to know them?

The probing questions: What are you thinking?

Getting to know our students serves many purposes; one of the most powerful is laying the foundation for questions that center on how our students are making sense of the content we share. When we invest time in understanding who our students are, we can incorporate that understanding as we pose questions that probe their relationship with what they are learning. By looking, in part, through their lens, we can pose additional questions designed to deepen their understanding and thinking about the topic. Some examples of these questions might be: How does this make sense to you? What is your understanding of the content? How would you describe this to another person? Why are we studying this content? What is the logical next step? How would you compare this topic to a topic you know well? How is this similar to what we talked about earlier? How is it different? How satisfied are you with your assignments, workload, experiment results, and so on?

The personal relevancy questions: So what?

Delving deeply with our students to ascertain their understanding of course content leads to the final type of questions—those that aim to assist students in taking the next giant step. This next step moves them from what they have learned into what they do with what they have learned. So much of the time, our heads are filled with content knowledge and skills. How we make sense of this knowledge and apply it determines the degree to which that content takes on new life of its own. The question "So what?" begs to be answered, as it prods the learner to think about the following: What am I going to do with this? How does it change my life? What difference will it make in the way I see the world? What difference will it make in the way I approach the world? What will I do differently? How does this change or affirm who I am? How will I move forward? What will be my next steps? What shifts in my life are occurring because of my shifts in thinking? Who am I now?

Final thoughts

Teaching offers countless opportunities for us to ask, inquire, probe, delve, dig, and uncover. But there are just as many opportunities for us to tell, recite, inform, lecture, share, and elucidate. In writing this, I am challenging myself and my colleagues to think about all those questions that are waiting to be posed. They are questions that can be loved, but not unless they are asked.

Reprinted from *The Teaching Professor,* October 2016

Group Work: Collaborative, Cooperative, or Problem-Based?

Maryellen Weimer, PhD

Recent interest in using group work to promote learning and develop important interpersonal skills began in the late '80s, and since then various types of group work have been promoted, researched, and implemented. Among the most widely used and best known "brands" are collaborative learning, cooperative learning, and problem-based learning. An outstanding article in a recent issue of the *Journal on Excellence in College Teaching* devoted to exploring group work looks in detail at these three approaches.

Despite widespread familiarity with the terms, collaborative, cooperative, and problem-based learning have been consistently muddled, mixed up, and used imprecisely to describe what students are doing in small groups. This inaccurate use of the terms has confounded practitioners' understanding of these forms of group work and the relationship between them.

Added to this definitional confusion is the fact that each of these forms of group work has had loyal advocates who've trumpeted one of the three over the other two. As a result, those who use cooperative learning or problem-based learning know little about collaborative learning. And those devoted to the collaborative approach don't use the other two. Few with an affinity for one of these three have much familiarity with the other two, and this exclusivity is one of the motivations for this article. Authors Neil Davidson and Claire Major wonder whether it's time for those using these three types of group work to start learning from each other. Their aim is not to be prescriptive, but descriptive. "What makes this article unique is its invitation to practitioners to cross traditional boundaries, to consider similarities and differences of these approaches, and to begin productive conversations that can advance the field of small-group learning." (p. 11)

These three approaches to group work do share certain features. Each starts with a common task or learning activity that can be completed by students working together in a group. Students talk (face-to-face or online) to each other about the task or activity they've been assigned to complete in each approach. They work together cooperatively. In each of these group structures, students are individually accountable for what they learn and what they contribute to the group's learning goal.

But each of these forms of group work has distinct features not shared by the others, and these differences are explored in lengthy detail in this article. Here's a nutshell summary of some of the features that make each unique. "Cooperative learning is more structured and employs more active teacher facilitation than collaborative learning." (p. 32) Problem-based learning is organized similarly to cooperative learning, with the key difference being its exclusive focus on problems. Collaborative learning relies on more open-ended interaction, with the goal being the discovery, understanding, or production of knowledge. (p. 21) In cooperative learning, roles may be assigned. They usually aren't in collaborative learning, and group interaction skills are not generally taught as part of collaborative learning activities. In cooperative learning, teachers usually form the groups, while in collaborative learning students form the groups themselves. Collaborative learning groups are mostly self-managed. Problem-based learning groups tend to be larger than the other two.

The use of these three forms of group work has followed disciplinary lines. Collaborative learning has been mostly used in the humanities and some in the social sciences but rarely in the sciences or professional programs. Cooperative learning has been mostly used in the sciences, math, engineering, the social sciences, and professional programs. Problem-based learning has been used across disciplines but was developed for use in medical education, and it is still most commonly associated with the health professions. The match between group structure and discipline has not received much attention in the literature. One could conjecture that the association derives from how knowledge in these disciplines is organized, how it is discovered, and how it advances.

The association between group work type and discipline has had other implications as well. Collaborative learning has not been studied much empirically, whereas cooperative learning and problem-based learning have received extensive empirical attention and with generally impressive results. The article highlights "strong evidence ... that students working in small groups outperform their counterparts in a number of key areas. These include knowledge development, thinking skills, social skills and course satisfaction." (p. 7)

In addition to the slim analysis of collaborative learning, the authors point out that research has not explored the optimal sequencing of group experiences. "We argue that exposing students to problem-solving learning in sequence from more structured to less structured will provide scaffolding to prepare them to succeed." (p. 45) They then offer a variety of ways this sequencing could be investigated.

Possibly the most compelling part of this article is how its analysis of the evidence clarifies the long-debated relations between these three forms of group work. "The cooperative learning approaches all employ certain elements which are not used by the collaborative teachers and which are not accepted by them. Hence, cooperative learning is not a form of collaborative learning (and vice versa). Likewise, problem-based learning is not a form of either. Cooperative learning, collaborative learning, and problem-based learning are all forms of small-group learning and have some major points in common. However, none of the approaches is a special case of any of the others." (p. 32) Table 2 on pages 33 and 34 lays out the differences and similarities that make each a related but separate form of group work.

The article reviews the literature and research of those who have advocated and studied each of these forms of group work. Ironically, many faculty who use group work are not familiar with either the advocates or the research. These are faculty who have learned to use group work the same way they learned to teach: by trial and error. They are using group work in ways that creatively integrate and combine these three (and other) approaches to group work, providing real-world examples of just how much advocates of a particular form of group work could be learning from each other.

Reference
Davidson, N., and Major, C. H. (2014). Boundary crossings: Cooperative learning, collaborative learning and problem-based learning. *Journal on Excellence in College Teaching, 25* (3 and 4), 7-55.

Reprinted from *The Teaching Professor,* November 2015

Designing Homework That Enhances Learning

Maryellen Weimer, PhD

What kind of homework assignments promote learning? We don't need research to confirm that doing homework benefits most (maybe it's all) college students. But there are some vexing issues. If the homework is graded and if those grades count, students will do the homework. But then all that homework must be graded. That can involve a huge time investment for the teacher. So, faculty respond by designing homework assignments that can be graded quickly or aren't graded at all, with students getting credit for completing them, provided the work shows they've made a reasonable effort. Both of those options tend to compromise the amount of learning that results from doing the homework assignment.

A faculty research team tested an interesting homework design feature in multiple sections of an undergraduate educational psychology course. Homework was assigned in every class session, and it consisted of 10 to 12 short-answer essay questions. Even though most of the questions could be answered in two to five sentences, that's enough homework grading to bury most teachers. In one of the experimental conditions, students simply got credit for the percentage of questions answered in each homework assignment—the completion option. In the other, answers to 10 percent of the questions (randomly selected) were graded according to quality criteria explained in the article. In this option, students knew some of their answers would be graded, they just didn't know which answers. The second approach reduced the instructor's grading time by 90 percent. Credit for both assignment options was the same.

Researchers were interested in two questions. "The first goal of the study was to determine if a randomized credit contingency [the second option] would produce higher-quality answers than assessment of all homework items for completion." (p. 65) "The second goal was to see if improvement in the quality of students' homework would indirectly improve their exam performance." (p. 65) And the results confirmed both these hoped-for conclusions. "Setting randomized reward contingencies specifically for accuracy of homework produced both significantly higher accuracy and length of homework answers than a reward contingency based on completion of the homework." (p. 73) The randomized answer option was also associated "with modest but significant gains in adjusted exam scores." (p. 73)

In a discussion of how these findings relate to other research, the study authors note that over the past decade, research has identified a number of factors that either contribute to or actually predict exam scores. They list (and reference) homework completion, critical-thinking ability, participation in class discussion, generic vocabulary, and student efficacy. "None of these studies considered separately constitute a dramatic contribution to exam scores, but taken together they provide a relatively extensive picture of what accounts for exam performance." (p. 74)

Completing a homework assignment like this one not only promotes the learning of course content, but it also brings students to class prepared to talk about the content. They can answer questions and add insights, and that makes for richer class discussions.

Design details, even small ones, do make a difference. In this case, they encouraged students to prepare longer and more accurate answers to questions about course material, and those answers were associated with better exam scores. And by reducing the number of answers that were graded, this design detail makes giving regular and substantial homework assignments a viable option for faculty members. Would students object to having to prepare answers for which they got no credit? In this case, exam questions were conceptually linked to the homework assignment questions. An example in the article illustrates this connection. If students are shown the relationship between homework questions and those on the exam, that may dampen their objections.

Reference
Galyon, C. E., Voils, K. L., Blondin, D. A., and Williams, R. L. (2015). The effects of randomized homework contingencies on college students' daily homework and unit exam performance. *Innovative Higher Education, 40* (1), 63-77.

Reprinted from *The Teaching Professor,* March 2015

Three Tips for Navigating Contentious Classroom Discussions

Rob Dornsife

Good teaching often relies on productive classroom discussion. However, many of us have experienced dynamics in which our discussions take a perilous turn and a palpable tension settles over the class. The precipitating comment may have offered a provocative perspective on an issue—maybe it rather aggressively challenged something someone said, or perhaps it smacked of racism, sexism, or some other discriminatory innuendo. Generally, students respond to comments they perceive as contentious with an awkward, uncomfortable silence. Nobody says anything; body language registers a collective recoil. What can or should teachers do when situations like this occur? Constructive disagreement, argument, and debate can play instrumental roles in learning, but not unless the exchange moves forward constructively. I'd like to offer three suggestions that can help teachers safely navigate through the potentially destructive terrains of contentious comments.

Remember that student investment is a crucial and desired resource. In my experience, contention in our classrooms usually results because the student cares. He or she has an investment in the idea or what's happened. Even contributions that are emotionally charged are offered because someone feels moved. We do well, first, to remember that caring engagement is a better and more readily engaged resource than complacency or indifference. So, our first step toward navigating contention is to recognize that more often than not, it results from a willingness to invest and engage. As such, it is a resource to be harnessed, not a tension to be feared.

Acknowledge the contention and define it as positively as possible.
How we define such occurrences goes a long way toward determining how
they are received. I will often end an animated and perilous discussion by
stating, overtly, how fortunate we are to have classmates this invested in
what we are discussing and how this kind of caring is at the root of our
shared inquiry. Crucial to this step is not ignoring or brushing aside
contention, pretending that we all agree when we don't, or that our
disagreements are small and inconsequential. Doing so risks heightening
the negative dynamics. Taking a moment or two to say something like
"the energy and investment demonstrated by your contributions is
really what this class should be all about" honestly redefines what may
otherwise be seen as something to be avoided rather than anticipated as
the class proceeds.

Use good spirit and humor to defuse contentious contributions.
I have found that well-placed, supportive humor defuses most potentially
negative energy. I recently had a young woman heatedly take issue with
the comments a young man made in the class. What followed was one of
those "silent" gasps, literally heard around the room. My default reaction
is respectful and honest humor. In this case, by combining suggestion two
with this one, I said something like "Wow, Mary, you really care about this.
We need to further unpack why and how this matters—and you are clearly
up to that task. But in the meantime, I would hate to lose to you in a poker
game! Now let's explore what you've said and why it matters." I believe that
humor often helps in these tension-filled situations.

Further, though often overlooked, the beginning and ending of the
class period afford teachers some special opportunities. They are more casual times and allow us a different sort of freedom to engage our students.
They are times when we can frame what will happen or has happened in
class. For example, if part of the class has taken one side and another part
has taken the opposite position, as they leave, I may, in a good-natured way,
suggest that if they see one another outside of class they should continue the
discussion. If a few students have gone after each other pretty aggressively, I
have said as they leave class that I'll buy the coffee if they'd like to meet and
talk through the issues more informally. Or, as the next class session begins,
I may remark on how our previous discussion really made me think—and
that I found it stimulating and look forward to more engaged exchanges as
the course proceeds.

These brief tips will not address the rare and extreme circumstances
that require different interventions. However, in my experience, such responses enable us to constructively handle the majority of those contentious

moments, transforming them into the healthy clash of different ideas and viewpoints we look forward to and depend on.

Reprinted from *The Teaching Professor,* February 2016

Facilitating Discussion

Maryellen Weimer, PhD

I t's another of those phrases frequently used and almost universally endorsed but not much talked about in terms of implementation. What does facilitating discussion mean? How should a teacher do it? Two faculty researchers, Finn and Schrodt (2016), frame the problem this way: "The literature is replete with descriptive accounts and anecdotal evidence but lacks the kinds of empirical investigations that could create theoretical coherency in this body of work." (p. 446) They decided our understanding of discussion facilitation could be deepened with an operational definition, one that resides in an instrument to measure it quantitatively.

Beyond developing and validating the instrument, they wondered what learning-related outcomes does discussion facilitation accomplish. Does it generate student interest and motivate learning? Can discussion promote those behaviors that reflect interest and involvement in learning across courses and in activities outside the classroom?

Developing the instrument was the first task. To do so they used literature on discussion to generate an initial pool of 75 items. Three hundred sixty undergraduates were asked to use those items to rate the discussion facilitation skills of the instructor they had in the course that met prior to the class in which the data were collected. Analysis of their responses revealed five factors involved in effective discussion facilitation.

- **Affirms students' discussion:** This aspect of discussion facilitation accounted for 45 percent of the variance, which was significantly higher than the other four factors. It included high ratings on items such as, "My teacher encourages participation during class discussions," "My teacher communicates appreciation for student contributions during discussion," and, "My teacher values what students say during class discussions." These data confirm a fundamental feature of effective discussion facilitation. Teachers must "patiently" and "positively" encourage students to contribute during discussion (p. 448).

- **Organizes discussion:** Discussions benefit from instructor guidance and direction, as long as they stop short of controlling the discussion. From the overall structure of the discussion, to promote the sense that it is going somewhere and to keep it on track, effective facilitation involves keeping the discussion focused on the designated topic. That focus needs to be achieved with guidance, a kind, constructive direction that sets the boundaries of the discussion without dictating or more subtly controlling what can be said within those boundaries. Participation in a discussion is dampened if there's a sense that participants aren't free to express relevant ideas, opinions, and perspectives.

- **Provokes discussion:** The skill here is sparking discussion with controversial statements (i.e., points that can be debated). The teacher needs to give students reasons to want to discuss something. Sometimes that's effectively accomplished when the teacher assumes a devil's advocate role. Interestingly, Finn and Schrodt (2016) found this factor generated mixed reactions from students. "Playing 'devil's advocate' with an air of inquisitiveness is quite different from playing 'devil's advocate' with an air of superiority." (p. 459) Discussion facilitation involves a nuanced use of verbal and nonverbal communication skills.

- **Questions students:** What you want to hear is, "My teacher asks students thought-provoking questions." Rather than questions with straightforward answers, these are open-ended, probing, even leading questions. When these kinds of questions are regularly infused throughout the discussion, they can help provide the structure a discussion needs. They can continue to provoke student interest, but, more importantly, they can make students think.

- **Corrects students:** Only accounting for 3.6 percent of the variance, this factor ended up being assessed with only three of the 33 items on the second version of the instrument. The idea here is that students appreciate teacher discussion facilitation that ensures that when it ends, they have information that is correct and enhances their understanding of course content.

As part of exploring the relationship between discussion facilitation and student interest and engagement, the researchers used a "student perceptions of instructor understanding" scale. It measures the extent to which students think instructors understand or misunderstand them, such as with, "My teacher understands the questions I ask." The second study documented that "when instructors provoke and organize discussions using a variety of questions, employ responses that affirm students, and correct discussions to focus on course content, such behaviors are directly associated with student interest and engagement in the course, as well as indirectly predictive of both outcomes through perceived understanding" (p. 459).

Not only is this instrument of value to subsequent explorations of discussion facilitation, it is a great tool for instructors who wish to understand the specific components of effective discussion facilitation. And for those interested in feedback on the extent to which they are effectively facilitating discussion, items on the final 25-item version of the instrument are included in the article. Kudos to these researchers for developing an instrument with both empirical and pragmatic utility. Best of all, it offers a clear description of how a teacher facilitates a discussion.

Reference
Finn, A. N., & Schrodt, P. (2016). Teacher discussion facilitation: A new measure and its associations with students' perceived understanding, interest and engagement. *Communication Education, 65*(4), 445–462.

Reprinted from *The Teaching Professor,* December 2016

Three Methods to Enhance Peer Review in Your Classroom

Amy Burden

We've all done it: asked students to switch papers before turning them in for editing and peer review, only to receive superficial comments and vague critiques that make us wonder if peer review is really worth the time. Some of us have students put sentences on the board for whole-class peer review. The sentences go up, but when I ask for edits that might make them better, I hear nothing but the crickets chirping.

Although extensive research indicates that peer review of student writing is beneficial and often critical to revision, many teachers are opting to leave it on the back burner. But I don't think it belongs there and would like to propose some ways technology can improve peer review. In fact, research is identifying a number of advantages from online peer review. The comments reviewers provide are easily read and printed. Students tend to maintain greater focus on the task in the online format. Teachers can monitor the discussions and weigh in as they see fit. Technology makes it easy to compare peer review drafts with finished papers to see progress. I've used the methods I'm describing here, and they are making peer review a more productive part of the writing process in my courses.

Facebook

Once you've created a separate account for work purposes, you can also create a "secret" group where you are the administrator. You simply add one student (whom you must "friend" temporarily) and ask that student to add others in the class.

Students can post specific writing assignments on the group "wall," indicating who they are so that the peer review can be personalized. From there, peers write comments on each post. The author can update his or her original posts to respond to feedback. This may promote further discussion and "replies" to comments. Using Facebook instead of an online learning platform such as Moodle or Blackboard enhanced participation by 50 percent among my students. It is a platform that students have access to 24/7; it alerts them when someone comments on their post and gives opportunities for a greater variety of feedback (video, comment, links, or reactions'). It's also free. Another feature for teachers is that peer reviews can be thoroughly monitored. Teachers have the ability to save, delete, and print all conversations.

Chat Rooms

If you do use online learning platforms such as Moodle or Blackboard, the chat room function works well for in-class peer review. Websites such as Edmodo provide the same type of chat room for free. Simply hook your laptop to a projector and invite students to use their smart devices to join you online. I ask targeted questions about what the students are writing and reading, and they provide verbal or typed feedback in real-time. It places all students at the front of the line for sharing their writing on the "board" quickly and efficiently. Additionally, these chats may be saved and printed.

Accountable Talk

So far, the two platforms I've discussed for using peer review save time in class and enhance levels of participation. However, they do not automatically improve the quality of the peer feedback. To achieve that goal, I've incorporated something proposed by Michaels and O'Connor called Accountable Talk (http://ifl.pitt.edu/index.php/educator_resources/ accountable_talk). They propose that students support their opinions with evidence using the following formula: "Student name" + critique + WHY using evidence. I pre-taught this approach by sharing example conversations with the phrases in bold that I wanted to be reproduced. I asked students specific questions about what they were reading and treated bolded phrases as vocabulary. I also created sentence frames and gave multiple practice opportunities to write responses in class. Students then worked in groups to practice verbal Accountable Talk with realistic situations. We worked on these phrases throughout the semester. I "liked" posts that used them correctly and brought these examples to the class's attention. When students used Accountable Talk, their edits went beyond grammar and spelling.

They referenced word choice and format and referred the writer back to the assignment, the textbook, and the grading rubric for evidence to support their opinions.

In my experiences, these three approaches have improved the quality of peer review in my courses. They use class time efficiently and encourage greater student participation. These technologies are also making my classroom more collaborative. I hope you'll consider how they might work in your writing assignments.

Reprinted from *The Teaching Professor,* December 2016

Student Presentations: Do They Benefit Those Who Listen?

Maryellen Weimer, PhD

Almost everyone agrees that student presentations benefit the presenter in significant ways. By doing presentations, students learn how to speak in front a group, a broadly applicable professional skill. They learn how to prepare material for public presentation, and practice (especially with feedback) improves their speaking skills. But those of us who have students do presentations in class know there's a downside—and that's how the rest of the class responds to these presentations. When the teacher talks, students more or less have to pay attention, at least some of the time, but when their classmates present, they can be comatose. Not only does this make it more difficult for the presenter, it means the students listening are not likely having any sort of learning experience.

Peer evaluations are one way to get students listening and learning from the presentations of others, as the authors of the article referenced below have documented. Students attend more carefully to what their classmates are saying when the evaluations they are doing "count." In this article, which describes the use of peer evaluations in ten 300-level political science courses, students evaluated every presentation and those evaluations constituted between 3 and 5 percent of their course grade—an amount the authors describe as "just enough to make the students take this assignment seriously." (p. 806) The quality of the feedback students provide is improved when they use criteria (in this case the same one the teachers used) to assess the presentations. Without much experience critiquing presentations and with no specific guidelines, they are likely to offer feedback that is generic and not particularly helpful, such as "Good presentation."

These authors had students in each of the 10 classes evaluate the peer evaluation assignment, and that feedback indicates the merit of having students do the evaluations. Seventy-three percent of the students agreed or strongly agreed that completing the evaluations made them pay more attention to the presentations. Almost 60 percent said doing the evaluations gave them a different perspective. "Students indicated they gained a different insight into the process, rather than just sitting through presentations without having any objective or direction as an audience member." (p. 806) Another sizable majority, almost 74 percent, agreed or strongly agreed that completing the evaluations clarified expectations for the presentation assignment.

Students were equally clear that they did not want the evaluations of their peers to have any role in determining their grade for the presentation. This response is interesting in light of the fact that an analysis of a subset of the data revealed a high correlation between instructor and student grades ($r = .740$). Instructor grades were slightly higher than student-assigned grades. Even though small, this difference was statistically significant. And even though students didn't want the assessment of their peers to count, over 80 percent agreed or strongly agreed that the feedback of peers would be helpful in improving subsequent presentations.

Peer evaluations can be used to increase the level of attention paid to presentations and the learning that might result from listening. They can also develop critiquing skills. Rather than incorporating peer critiques into the grade of the presenter, maybe part or all of the critique grade could be determined by the presenter, who rates the quality of the feedback provided. Sometimes the logistics of peer evaluations discourage faculty from using them—multiple evaluations to collect, record, sort, and return. What about an online system of peer reviews? Or assign a certain number of peer reviewers to each presentation. That ensures that at least a portion of the audience are attending, and with fewer evaluations to prepare, students could be expected to provide more detailed feedback. Or how about some bonus points to the students whose presentations are rated highest by their colleagues? The details associated with using peer evaluations can be handled in a variety of interesting and useful ways.

Reference
Baranowski, M., and Weir, K. (2011). Peer evaluation in the political science classroom. *PS, Political Science and Politics, 44* (4), 805-811.

Reprinted from *The Teaching Professor,* January 2012

Writing Comments That Lead to Learning

Susan M. Taylor

Instructors who require papers spend a good deal of time emphasizing the importance of audience and purpose in writing. Writers who remember their readers and their writing objectives are much more likely to use good judgment about the decisions that go into creating an effective piece of writing. This is equally true of the comments instructors write on students' papers. I'd like to share some suggestions, some of which I learned the hard way.

Students often react first to the number of comments on the paper. They look to see how much the instructor "bled" on their papers. They may not even read overall comments that appear at the end. Sometimes it helps to put those comments up front so that students see them first.

Notes in the margins of the papers tend to be sketchy. With little room in the margins, instructors use more underlining, coding, and abbreviating. Many marginal notes simply label a problem without further explanation or example. For instance, I have written, "There are stronger works for your POV" on papers not thinking that POV (for point of view) may be an unfamiliar acronym. Not only does this feedback puzzle and frustrate students, it doesn't help them improve.

There is a difference between an explanation that simply shows the students how to reword or rewrite something and an in-depth explanation that discusses the reasoning behind the suggested change. For example, in a legal brief for my Business Law class, a student wrote, "This is an appeal from the judgment of the St. Joseph County Superior Court, by a jury, that the defendant was guilty of check forgery." After having spent so much time on the papers that my hand ached, I gave into writer's cramp and simply underlined "the judgment" and "by the jury." Fortunately, the student came to me and asked what I meant.

On one of my first papers (when my hand was fresh and cramp free), I wrote, "Watch your language. A jury convicts or acquits but cannot render a judgment. The court enters a judgment on the jury's verdict." This comment is a more useful explanation.

Instructors must balance the positive and negative comments, remembering the importance of positive feedback. It motivates students, is essential to improvement, and builds confidence. If students are told why something is good, they can do more of it subsequently. Papers lacking any positive feedback tend to lead to poor student morale.

Closely related is the overall tone of the comments. Instructors need to keep the tone professional. Constructive criticism goes a long way, but destructive criticism goes an even longer way. Once someone destroys your self-confidence as a writer, it is almost impossible to write well.

How many is too many? Instructors should monitor the number of comments they write on students' papers. Although it may be tempting to comment on everything, the workload quickly becomes intolerable and too much feedback may overwhelm the students. They find it difficult to prioritize the comments and tend to retreat into simple and safe writing in an effort to avoid another barrage of comments. Or they don't even read the comments and therefore learn nothing from the feedback. However, the major problem with the over-commented paper is that the instructor has lost both a sense of focus and a point of view.

The solution is to separate the mechanical comments and the substantive comments. The mechanical comments encourage the student to see the paper as a fixed piece that just needs some editing. The substantive comments, however, suggest that the student still needs to develop the meaning by doing more research.

When commenting on students' papers, think of your audience and your purpose. Your job as an instructor is to reach your students to help them learn and grow. If your comments do not accomplish your goal, then it doesn't matter how much time and effort you put into the papers.

Reprinted from *The Teaching Professor,* October 2009

Making the Review of Assigned Reading Meaningful

Sarah K. Clark

The typical college student dreads hearing, "Let's review the chapters you read for homework." What generally ensues is a question and answer drill in which students are peppered with questions designed to make clear who has and hasn't done the reading. In reality, these exchanges do little to encourage deep thought or understanding of the assigned reading. They produce awkward silences during which students squirm in their seats, hoping to become invisible. Other times students decline to answer for fear of giving the wrong answer. Almost all the time a negative tone permeates the classroom during this review. I decided to restructure the way that I approached reviews of reading assignments, and found that by doing things differently, I could change both the tone and outcomes of the review activity. I'd like to share some of the ideas and techniques that I have found useful:

The Top Ten: Ask students to create their own "Top Ten List" of important concepts presented in the chapter(s). I encourage student collaboration in the creation of these lists. The activity provides a nice review of the material, and you'll be amazed at what students consider to be most important. I use these lists as a starting point for discussions. They also let me know what areas of content need further explanation. For students who didn't do the reading, the lists expose them to ideas in the text and that prepares them at least a bit for the subject of the day.

Secondary Sources: Gone are the days when the textbook is the only source of information available to students. With blogs, research articles, journals, informational pages, and news websites at the touch of a fingertip, students can easily learn more about the subject. After they've done the assigned readings, have students locate another viewpoint on the subject and bring it to class. In class, set a time limit (say 15 minutes) and have partners/groups discuss the reading material and their secondary sources. As you circulate around the room, you may hear some good examples that you can use later in the period. Interestingly, students often (without being asked) continue to bring in outside resources on the topics we study, which makes for rich and healthy discussions.

Journaling: For the ideas presented in the readings to become relevant, students need to articulate thoughts about what they are reading and they need to hear how others responded as well. I encourage my students to write journal notes, which I describe as what the brain is thinking while reading. Example: "Wow! I never considered how George Washington must have felt during this turbulent time in the nation's history. I always thought of him as liking his role as president." Students can share their journaling with a partner or small group. This exercise helps students get past initial impressions, and it connects what they already know to the new information.

Divide and Conquer: Divide up the next reading chapter among small groups of students. Student A reads the first section in the chapter, Student B reads the next section, and so forth. The next day, students meet in small groups and report on the section they read. Or you can have groups of students that read the same section meet with students who read different sections. Students become dependent on one another to create the full picture of what was in the reading material. My students seem to enjoy these group discussions, which are a way to become familiar with the material before being graded on it.

Using these and other strategies has really made a difference in my classes. More students are engaged in and contributing to class discussions, and they are moving beyond a simple repetition of facts and details. Students are digging deeper and connecting their world with other viewpoints, and that gives them a richer understanding of the content.

These new approaches are having an effect on me, too. I am more calm and confident in my role as a teacher and a learner. I find it easier to be more patient and thoughtful with my students. Most important, I have noticed that the classroom feels like a safe and positive place. Students show greater respect for one another and more appreciation of the material. In my opinion, all these responses make these changes worthwhile!

Reprinted from *The Teaching Professor,* November 2010

Helping Students Memorize: Tips from Cognitive Science

Michelle Miller, PhD

I was wrapping up a presentation on memory and learning when a colleague asked, "How do we help students learn in courses where there's a lot of memorization?" He explained that he taught introductory-level human anatomy, and although the course wasn't *all* memorization, it did challenge students' capacity to retain dozens of new terms and concepts.

The question itself is tricky because most teaching professionals are heavily invested in the idea that learning isn't about being able to regurgitate facts on an exam. We also worry, and with good reason, that emphasizing rote learning steals time and effort away from the deeper thinking that we want students to do. But in my work I've come to realize that memorization deserves some airtime because it is one important route to building content knowledge and expertise. Furthermore, acquiring content knowledge doesn't have to detract from critical thinking, reasoning, or innovation—rather, it can complement all these. Cognitive scientists are making new discoveries all the time about the connections between memory and processes such as drawing inferences, making predictions, and other skills that make up the ability to think like an expert in a discipline.

So what techniques target this specific teaching and learning challenge? We're all familiar with mnemonics such as the first-letter technique—using a word such as RICE (rest, ice, compression, elevation) or a catchy phrase (Every Good Boy Does Fine) to remember a sequence of information. Mnemonics are one good tool, but what else can we offer?

For starters, we should convey to students (and keep in mind ourselves) that memorization challenges nearly everyone because the mind simply isn't set up to take in reams of disjointed facts. Our memory systems evolved to be picky about what we remember, selecting the information that is most relevant to our goals and discarding the rest. Understanding this helps us and our students have realistic expectations about the level of effort needed to succeed.

It also helps to understand how we create memories for words, because many memorization tasks involve scientific terms, foreign language vocabulary, and the like. How we do this has been hotly debated among researchers, but one view is that we rely on a special piece of mental machinery called the *phonological loop* that holds speech sounds.

If you've ever muttered a phone number to yourself while you ran around looking for a pencil to write it down with, you've experienced the phonological loop in action. But recycling phone numbers isn't the phonological loop's main reason for existing. Rather, its real job kicks in when we run into a word we haven't heard before. When this happens, the phonological loop grabs onto the sequence of sounds and keeps it fresh while other memory systems set up representations of what the new word means. The catch is that phonological loop capacity varies fairly substantially from individual to individual. This means that words of three, four, or more syllables overwhelm some people's ability to learn new words on the fly.

With these two points in mind—that memory doesn't handle disjointed facts well and new vocabulary hinges on one sometimes-shaky mechanism within memory—here are some ways to help students manage memorization:

- Emphasize **context and purpose**. Ask yourself why students are being asked to memorize these facts in the first place. If students can readily answer that question and if they can picture future situations in which they will use the information, they will be better primed to remember it.
- **Break down** new vocabulary words, especially those that are more than two syllables long. Allow time to rehearse and remember the first couple of syllables before tacking on later ones. Also keep in mind that this process will be easier for some students than others due to wide variation in phonological loop capacity; you may want to design in a "mastery learning" or other individualized approach for vocabulary so that students can move through at their own pace.
- **Visualize** information. For most people, imagery is highly memorable, perhaps because so much of the brain is devoted to visual processing. Memory champions, such as the ones populating the best seller *Moonwalking with Einstein*, use elaborate visualization strategies to achieve incredible feats of memorization. Similarly, strategies

such as the *keyword mnemonic* work by linking word sounds to images (such as using an image of a cowboy on a horse to remember the Spanish word "caballo," which sounds a bit like "cowboy").

• Take advantage of the "Big Three" applied memory principles—**testing, spacing, and interleaving**. Briefly, these refer to the facts that quizzes are a great way to study and that we do best when we spread out our study sessions and alternate between different topics. Tackling a big memory project such as human anatomy means we need every advantage we can get, and dozens of research studies have supported these three as producing the biggest memory payoff for the time invested.

• Avoid the **rereading trap**. Students tend to fall into passively reviewing material, and in doing so they miss the key advantage of techniques such as testing: *retrieval practice*. Retrieval practice strengthens memory, but it works only when we actively challenge memory. Flash cards, a favorite student strategy, are fine as long as students use them to actively quiz themselves.

It's okay to expect students to learn the facts and terms needed to become experts in a discipline. With an understanding of memory and some strategies to share, we can make this side of learning productive and maybe even painless—but certainly at least less painful.

Reprinted from *The Teaching Professor,* November 2014

PART 3

•

Testing and Evaluation

Does Dropping or Replacing the Lowest Exam Score Detract from Learning?

Maryellen Weimer, PhD

It's a practice that's used by a number of faculty, across a range of disciplines, and in a variety of forms. Sometimes the lowest exam score is simply dropped. In other cases, there's a replacement exam and the score on that exam can be used instead of any exam score that's lower. It's a strategy used with quizzes probably a bit more often than with exams.

The reasons for doing so include the perennial problem of students missing test events—sometimes for good reasons and other times not—but what teacher wants to adjudicate the reasons? It's also a practice that responds to test anxiety—some students find testing situations so stressful they aren't able to demonstrate their understanding of the material.

There are arguments against the strategy. Some contend that it contributes to grade inflation. Others worry that knowing the lowest score will be dropped motivates strategic test taking: students don't study for a test or quiz, deciding beforehand that it will be their lowest score and they will drop or replace it subsequently. This means there's a chunk of material that they have learned less well. Another downside of a replacement or makeup exam is the extra time and energy involved in writing and grading it.

But what do we know about the practice empirically? Very little, it turns out. Raymond MacDermott, who has done several empirical explorations of the practice, found little related work in his review of the literature. In this study he looked at the effects of three alternatives on cumulative final exam scores in a microeconomics course: three exams, each worth 20 percent of the grade, and a cumulative final worth 40 percent of the grade;

three exams, with the lowest score dropped, and the cumulative final counting for 40 percent; and three exams, each worth 20 percent, with a cumulative replacement exam, offered at the end of the course, which could be used to replace the lowest score on one of the three exams, plus the regular cumulative final worth 40 percent of the grade. The study took place across multiple sections of the course, all taught by MacDermott, with the content, instructional methods, and test types remaining the same.

The results are interesting. Dropping the lowest test score did not compromise performance on the cumulative final. "Contrary to previous research and conventional wisdom . . . allowing students to drop their lowest grade improved performance on a cumulative final exam, while offering a replacement test had no significant effects." (p. 364) These findings resulted even though there was some evidence of strategic test taking. Some students who performed well on two of the tests had a significantly lower score on the third one. MacDermott believes that did not impact the final exam score because the final was cumulative. Students knew they would be tested on all the course content. The replacement exam, also cumulative, was formatted differently than other tests in the course (multiple-choice questions versus short answers and problems), and MacDermott wonders whether that may have hindered student performance.

Because research on these practices is limited and they are used in many different iterations, generalizations from this work to other fields, content, and students are not in order. The analysis MacDermott employed is straightforward and could be replicated. Faculty who are using (or considering using) one of these approaches should verify its effectiveness with evidence. As MacDermott points out, "The true question with each [approach] should regard the impact on student learning. While the student may appreciate the opportunity to drop their lowest grade, does it lead to behavior that may detract from learning?" (p. 365) In this study it did not, but is that true across the board? Is it true given other iterations of the approach? Does its impact depend on the content, test question format, or course level? These questions and others merit our attention.

Reference
MacDermott, R. J. (2013). The impact of assessment policy on learning: Replacement exams or grade dropping. *Journal of Economic Education, 44* (4), 364-371.

Reprinted from *The Teaching Professor,* August 2015

Testing That Promotes Learning

Maryellen Weimer, PhD

Testing has a prominent role in most college courses. It's the method most often used to determine the extent to which students have mastered the material in the course. Say "tests" and thoughts jump immediately to evaluation and grades, with students thinking "stressful" simultaneously or shortly thereafter. What rarely crosses the minds of students and teachers is the power of testing to promote learning. Cynthia J. Brame, PhD, and Rachel Biel, CFT, in their article, *Test-enhanced learning: The potential for testing to promote greater learning in undergraduate science courses,* noted that "One of the most consistent findings in cognitive psychology is that testing leads to increased retention more than studying alone does." (p. 1)

Testing, as it's understood by teachers and students, "does not reflect the setting in which the benefits of 'test-enhanced learning' have been experienced. In the experiments done in cognitive science laboratories, the 'testing' was simply a learning activity for students." (p. 9) It was "no stakes" (as in it didn't count in grade calculation) or "low stakes" (as in it counted very little). Brame and Biel think "retrieval practice" might be a more accurate description of the activity involved here.

The article highlights research that documents six positive benefits achieved by this kind of testing. They are derived from studies that involved undergraduates "learning educationally relevant materials (e.g., text passages as opposed to word pairs)." (p.1) Here's a brief synopsis of each effect. They are described in much greater detail in the article with highlights from individual studies and an elaborate table.

Repeated retrieval enhances long-term retention in a laboratory setting. When you learn something new, the more times you retrieve the information, the better you remember it. Studies here document that repeated testing (which is all about retrieval) facilitated long-term retention better than studying did. In other words, testing oneself with questions is more effective than just going over the material.

Various testing formats can enhance learning. The questions can be multiple choice; they can be short answer, cued recall, even free recall. Various questions types have been shown to provide significant benefit over study alone.

Feedback enhances the benefits of testing. Simply answering questions did improve performance, but feedback, as in finding out the correct answer, provided an added benefit.

Learning is not limited to rote memory. To some faculty, test-enhanced learning may seem like the kind of testing that encourages students to just memorize material. The authors discuss research here that identifies benefits beyond simple recall, such as being able to transfer knowledge to different domains.

Testing potentiates further study. The case in point here is pretesting and research documenting that it improves students' studying, perhaps by cuing them to focus on key ideas.

The benefits of testing appear to extend to the classroom. All of the research highlighted in support of the previous five benefits was conducted in laboratories. However, there are studies suggesting "the benefits of testing may also extend to the classroom." (p. 8)

The authors conclude with a section that suggests some ways faculty might consider implementing what is known about test-enhanced learning.

More and frequent quizzing. "The studies summarized earlier suggest that providing students the opportunity for retrieval practice—and ideally, providing feedback for the responses—will increase learning of targeted and related material." (p. 10)

Providing "summary points" during a class. This approach encourages retrieval practice by asking students to use their words to recall key or main points at various intervals during a class period and/or at its conclusion. Their summaries could be written in their notes, shared with those nearby, or spoken in class.

Use of pretesting. Testing students' prior knowledge of a subject appears to "prime" them for learning. These tests could be administered at the beginning of a unit or class session or online with a question set that students could be told they will need to be able to answer after learning the material.

Sharing what is known about test-enhanced learning. The recommendation here is to talk with students about this kind of testing, explaining how it has been shown to enhance learning. It will be a new way for students to think about testing, but it's certainly a more positive and less stressful take on the value of test questions and testing experiences.

Kudos to the authors for undertaking this review and putting together an article that makes the findings understandable and useful to practitioners. It's one of those pieces of scholarship prepared for faculty in one discipline that can be used to make teaching more evidence-based in any field.

Reference
Brame, C. J. & Biel, R., (2015). Test-enhanced learning: The potential for testing to promote greater learning in undergraduate science courses. *Cell Biology Education—Life Sciences Education, 14* (Summer), 1-12.

Reprinted from *The Teaching Professor,* October 2015

Making the Grading Process More Transparent

Maryellen Weimer, PhD

College teachers are always on the look-out for ways to help students better understand why their paper, essay answer, or project earned a particular grade. Many students aren't objective assessors of their own work, especially when there's a grade involved, and others can't seem to understand how the criteria the instructor used applies to their work.

As the author Matthew Bamber notes, grading is not a transparent process to students, even if they have been given the criteria or rubric beforehand. He devised an exercise for his master's-level accounting and finance students that they found "eye-opening." In the UK, students "sit" for lengthy exams—in this case, a three-hour, closed-book essay test. In the exercise, students began by answering one lengthy essay question. When finished, they were given a suggested answer to the question (it contained a problem they had to solve and a written analysis), a marking guide, and a set of grade descriptors. Then they were given an anonymous answer to the same question and told to grade it using the materials provided. After having completed that step, students were given a teacher-graded copy of the anonymous answer. The exercise concluded with students being told to grade their answer to the question.

What an experience for students! You can see why they'd call it eye-opening. Adaptation of the whole exercise or parts of it could profitably be used during exam review sessions. Students could work individually or in groups with a problem or an essay question, maybe one from an exam used in a previous course. The grading criteria or a rubric will be helpful when students have little or no experience grading exam answers or other kinds of written work. The exercise is made powerful when the grades given by the students are compared with those given by the teacher and students can see how the teacher has applied the grading criteria differently than they did. In the case of these accounting-finance students, they saw not only the final score but also how the instructor scored the various parts of the answer.

If students are new to grading, it may be better to start by having them look at an anonymous answer first. Author-instructor Bamber notes that the quality of the answer students grade is important. If it's a superstar answer with little that needs correcting, students may not learn much from the process. On the other hand, they may not learn very much if the answer is poor and does not exemplify any aspects of a good answer. In his case, instructor Bamber chose an answer in the midrange.

Early on as well, students may benefit from group collaborations. They can start by making an individual assessment of the answer. Then when they convene as a group, those individual assessments can be shared and used to generate a group assessment of the answer. This gives students the opportunities to hear how others read and responded to the answer.

The idea of having students look at their own work with the objective of grading it is the kind of experience that begins to develop accurate assessment abilities. The accounting-finance students were surprisingly accurate in their assessment of their answers after having graded the anonymous one. Obviously, this part of the exercise must be designed so that it encourages students to be honest. It's not about the grade they want but the one they think their work deserves. Here too, having the criteria, rubrics, or checklists is helpful. An incentive may be necessary as well, since students may not see any reason to take the activity seriously. Whatever grade they give their answer doesn't count.

The accounting-finance students in this article gained an appreciation for the grading process. "Many indicated their surprise at the amount of time, energy and concentration that this exercise required of them." (p. 480) They also expressed concerns about the integrity of the process when teachers have many answers to grade. The instructor concludes, "The findings suggest that this exercise has the potential to enhance participants' understanding of a subject as well as its assessment criteria." Even though the exercise as described here probably can't be replicated in most North American courses, adaptations of it can. The exercise in various iterations has the potential to make the assessment of graded work more transparent to students.

Reference

Bamber, M., (2015). The impact of stakeholder confidence of increased transparency in the examination assessment process. *Assessment & Evaluation in Higher Education, 40* (4), 471-487.

Reprinted from *The Teaching Professor,* January 2016

The Case for Reading Quizzes

Maryellen Weimer, PhD

With most instructional practices, it's all about how they're implemented. That's what determines whether they're right or wrong. Professor Tropman teaches introductory and upper division philosophy courses. She acknowledges that there are arguments against using reading quizzes, but writes, "I have had success using quizzes in my classes." (p. 145) "For me, quizzes help set the atmosphere that I seek: one with the expectation that everyone comes to class prepared to engage with the material at hand." (p. 143)

Here's a quick rundown as to how she uses reading quizzes. Students find out about them on the first day of class. "I explain to my students that reading philosophy is crucial to learning, writing, and doing philosophy." (p. 141) Her students don't have a reading quiz every day, but quizzes happen often enough that students know they need to arrive in class having done the reading. To get students accustomed to these quizzes and to help them know how to prepare, she launches the activity with several non-graded, noncollected practice quizzes.

And she uses different kinds of quizzes. Sometimes the one or two quiz questions can be answered with a few words; sometimes answers require a sentence or two. Some days she solicits students' critical reflections on the reading; other days they are asked to summarize the main points in the reading. On occasion students complete the quiz in pairs or in groups. Some days the quizzes are open-book. A handful are even take-home. If the reading is particularly challenging, she may give students a reading question with the assignment. If they come to class able to answer that question, they will do well on the quiz question.

She underscores the importance of the reading by making the quizzes worth 20 percent of the grade in the introductory course and 15 percent in the upper division course. She does give partial credit for answers, but no credit for an answer that indicates the student has not read the material or has only skimmed it. Makeups aren't allowed, but the lowest two quiz scores are dropped at the end of the course.

Reading quizzes in these courses garner a range of benefits. Students come to class and on time, as the reading quizzes are the opening activity. As they wait for class to begin, students are reviewing the reading and talking about it with each other. "Not surprisingly, since many students come to class already familiar with the text at hand, and having thought about the reading, class discussion is much more fruitful and lively." (p. 141)

This article is exceptional in that Professor Tropman deals with the arguments against quizzing. She describes them in detail, including quotations, and then she responds—with reasons and accounts of her own experiences. For example, some have argued that regularly quizzing fosters antagonistic relationships between the teacher and the class. Students become resentful. Professor Tropman admits she shared this concern the first semester she used quizzes. "Yet, rather than facing a class revolt, I found students are grateful for quizzes." (p. 143) And the data she collected from students in both courses confirms this. Of the students surveyed, 89 percent reported a very positive or somewhat positive overall opinion of the quizzes. Did the quizzes encourage them to do the reading? Eight-five percent said they did so at a high or moderate level. Undoubtedly, the way Professor Tropman administers the quizzing activity contributes to this positive response.

Perhaps the most compelling argument against reading quizzes is that they motivate students to read for the wrong reasons. They are reading to get the quiz points, and that contributes to grade-oriented attitudes rather than learning-oriented approaches. Professor Tropman recognizes the validity of the argument but suggests that quizzes might increase intrinsic motivation. "To the extent that quizzes help improve one's reading skills, reading will become less frustrating, as well as more enjoyable, rewarding, and stimulating." (p. 144) And then this point: "Once students are able to see a real connection between the day's reading and classroom discussion, difficult texts can become less foreign and more accessible." (p. 144) Maybe students would need less "force" to do the reading if they understood how much reading (in most courses) promotes their understanding of the course content.

It's a well-written article that underscores how teaching strategies are not definitively right or wrong. How well they work depends on how they're used. In this case the professor includes many quiz features that promote learning and engagement. She also includes components that lessen the anxiety students often associate with testing situations. Success of instructional strategies also depends on the context in which they're used. As one of Professor Tropman's students candidly observed of the philosophy course, "I can't see how this class would function without the reading quizzes." (p. 143)

Reference
Tropman, E. (2014). In defense of reading quizzes. *International Journal of Teaching and Learning in Higher Education, 26* (1), 140-146.

Reprinted from *The Teaching Professor,* March 2016

The Value of Rubrics for Teachers

Maryellen Weimer, PhD

Rubrics clarify assignment details for students. They provide an operational answer to the frequently asked student question, "What do you want in this assignment?" They make grading more transparent and can be used to help students develop those all-important self-assessment skills. For teachers, rubrics expedite grading and can make it a more objective process.

But there's another benefit for teachers that's not often mentioned, and that's the power of rubrics to clarify thinking about the knowledge and skills the teacher wants to assess. Teachers do a great deal of assessment, across multiple courses, semester after semester. It's easy for the response to student work to become habitual, automatic, and not always thoughtful. After grading so many hundreds of essays and short answers, the good, the bad, and the ugly are easy to pick out.

The process of creating a rubric forces close consideration of what is being assessed—its parts, features, or characteristics. It also promotes clearer understanding of what a performance or product looks like when it's not right, only partly accomplished, good enough as it is, or everything it ought to be. With rubrics, teachers can not only quickly identify different quality levels, they know why an essay or answer belongs in that category.

Rubrics can be simple or detailed to the nth degree, but they don't have to be complex to be beneficial. Here's an example that illustrates a discussion-group rubric used by a history teacher in an online course. She writes that she adapted it from another source. Here are two of the four categories on the rubric.

A or A - : Timely discussion contributions. Comments are meaningful and show preparedness that reflect course readings. In-depth thought and contributions add to the overall learning of other individuals in the course. Demonstrations of courtesy and respect to others.

C+ to C - : Overall contributions are not meaningful and include types of comments such as "good idea" or "I agree." Very little evidence of having read course materials or giving any in-depth thought to the reading. Failure to participate in at least two discussions during the posting period.

Rubrics can be beneficial in any aspect of instruction—an in-class activity, a major assignment, a teacher's quizzing strategy, a course, and probably most beneficial of all, the levels of learning resulting from a sequence of courses or a whole major or program.

Here's a second example. A group of chemists worked with teaching staff to develop an assessment strategy that would help them understand "the extent to which students were able to think critically about or solve laboratory-based problems across the curriculum, with particular attention to the application of chemical instrumentation." (p. 319) They opted to develop a rubric because "cognitive skills, such as critical thinking or problem solving are difficult to measure with a conventional 'test,' graded for correct vs. incorrect answers." (p. 319) Their rubric is anchored around these three criteria:

1. It identifies the important or relevant features of the problem.
2. In formulating a strategy for the solution of the problem, the student presents a complete justification or explanation for the strategy.
3. It provides an effective strategy that is likely to work to solve the chemical problem.

For each criterion, emerging, developing, and mastering levels are described.

Teachers can create rubrics alone and achieve the benefits described here, but chances are good those benefits will be achieved on a much bigger scale if developing the rubric is a collaborative process. Say a group of teachers in a department or program aspire to develop students' critical-thinking skills. What are the identifying features of those skills? At what different levels might they occur on the way to full development? Even if those teachers don't end up agreeing on all parts of the rubric, the conversation will likely have been a rich learning experience for all involved. And if a rubric is mutually acceptable, then teachers with a shared goal are working from the same playbook.

References
Shadle, S. E., Brown, E. C., Towns, M. H., & Warner, D. L., (2012) A rubric for assessing students' experimental problem-solving ability. *Journal of Chemical Education,* 89 (3), 319–325.
Stern, A., (2015) Bridging the gap: Replicating the interactivity of the physical classroom in an online environment. *The History Teacher,* 48 (3), 483–504.

Reprinted from *The Teaching Professor,* April 2016

Using Evaluation Results to Improve: What Does It Take?

Maryellen Weimer, PhD

Teachers don't always have the best attitudes about student rating results, and for reasons that are clearly understandable. Institutions often don't evaluate teaching in the most constructive and useful ways. However, feedback from students is an essential part of any effort to grow and develop as a teacher. Here are some research results that shed light on ways teachers can approach rating results that make them a useful part of improvement efforts.

It pretty much starts and ends with having the right attitude, and these researchers offer an array of alternatives that describe what they mean by "attitude." They suggest the term "approach"—how you approach evaluation results. They also propose "perception," "perspective," "stance," "belief," or "conception." (p. 1) "The question we address is: what attitude or approach do teachers take to their student evaluations so that they can use them for formative or developmental purposes, to improve their teaching rather than to give a final assessment of performance?" (p. 2)

To answer the question, they gathered information from experienced, award-winning teachers during two-hour focus group sessions. They used a semistructured interview process during which they asked questions like these: What overall attitudes do you need to use evaluation data to improve teaching? How do you interpret or analyze the evaluations? How do you decide what to do on the basis of the evaluations? How do you decide what changes to make on the basis of the evaluations?" (p. 4).

What emerged out of these focus group discussions was what the researchers labeled an "improvement attitude . . . an overarching approach, perspective, orientation, or way of looking at evaluation data" (p. 5) which they organized into four "interrelated, overlapping, smaller categories for ease of discussion." (p. 5)

Reflective Approach

This part of the approach begins with a simple question: "How can I improve?" The question is asked regularly; the pursuit of improved teaching is ongoing. Often what drives this question is basic curiosity—the need to find out what's going on in one's courses or always being on the lookout for ways to improve student learning.

The drive for improvement is not predicated on notions of remediation or deficiency. It's not about needing to improve because the teaching still isn't good enough. Too often, evaluation results are perused in order to identify what needs to be fixed. Another author cited in this article calls this the "fire alarm" approach, the belief that rating results are relevant only when there's a fire in the course that needs to be put out. The alternative proposed by those interviewed in the study is the notion that there's always room for improvement—it doesn't matter how good you are, or if you aren't all that good. The reflective approach is also tied up in thinking about current practice and not being so vested in what you do that you can't possibly consider changing it.

Data Viewed as Formative Feedback

From this perspective, the feedback students provide is not a judgment of the teacher or the teaching. It's simply feedback. Two questions illustrate the different perspective here: "How can I develop and improve my teaching?" rather than "How good is my teaching?" (p. 7).

If the focus is on the second question, then there's often a need to explain away the results or to blame them on students, the course, or one's teaching circumstances. A focus on the second question also makes it easier to simply ignore the results—the teaching is good enough, there's no need to improve. In contrast, participants with an improvement attitude "focused on how they could use the data to improve, rather than paying attention to how they could explain the data away." (p. 7) All student feedback should be taken seriously and given careful consideration. As one teacher put it bluntly, "I'm right and 1,300 students are wrong? I don't think so." (p. 7)

Avoiding excuses did not mean these teachers ignored reasons associated with the results. Rather, they could be used to explain some of the results. Required courses often generate student complaints. But that's not where these teachers focused their attention. They were trying to figure out what the results meant, what they could learn from them about their teaching and about student learning experiences in the course. "If students give less than perfect ratings or negative feedback, this indicates that something is not working for them and so there is room for improvement." (p. 8)

Belief in the Ability to Improve

"When teachers adopted the improvement attitude, they thought they could improve their teaching, they could make a difference for student learning, and they could improve their evaluations, rather than these all being unchangeable." (p. 8)

Participants in the study did agree that some of this confidence comes with experience. It's not as easy to take negative feedback and to believe in your ability to make things better when your teaching experience is limited.

Student-Centered Approach

Again, two questions differentiate the improvement attitude from an attitude that becomes a barrier to improvement: "How well have my students learned?" versus "How well have I taught?" (p. 9) According to the study authors, "The teachers saw the evaluation data not just as shining a light on themselves and what they have done, but as shining a light on their students: what benefits and blocks their learning? How well are they enabled and supported to learn?" (p. 9) Fundamentally, these teachers' thinking is more about learning and less about teaching.

However, it's not as simple and straightforward as teachers doing whatever students suggest. Sometimes what students want isn't what they need. What they suggest won't improve their learning in the course. But what students want and what they think they need still merits consideration and response. If students are largely opposed to essay questions on exams, but the teacher has good reasons to believe that's the best way to promote deep learning of course concepts, then it would be irresponsible to give students what they want. In such a case, the teacher must explain the educational rationale behind this choice of exam question and may want to explore with students what else could happen in the course that would help them prepare for essay questions.

This is a very fine article. It articulates an attitude that makes rating results useful. Attitudes are not immutable. They can be changed and developed, and if there is a place in higher education where attitudes could benefit from change, faculty response to course evaluations is it. For a variety of reasons, many teachers don't have good attitudes about student ratings. This work shows a clear path to a more useful, positive, and constructive way of thinking about course evaluation feedback from students.

Reference
Golding, C., and Adam, L. (2016). Evaluate to improve: Useful approaches to student evaluation. *Assessment & Evaluation in Higher Education, 41*(1), 1–14.

Reprinted from *The Teaching Professor,* September 2016

Grading Practices: More Subjective Than Objective?

Maryellen Weimer, PhD

A recent survey of 175 economics professors who teach basic principles of economics courses revealed a widely diverse set of grading practices for the course. These instructors taught at 118 different institutions, including doctoral degree-granting universities, two-year colleges, and everything in between. The findings are specific to the course and the field of economics. However, the questions raised by the analysis are relevant to grading across the board. The different grading policies and practices reported here are not uncommon, and one would suspect that findings like these are typical of any number of courses routinely offered by our institutions.

Giving grades vs. earning grades: The authors begin by pointing out that the usual decree that faculty don't "give" grades, students "earn" them is not entirely accurate. The decree makes it sound as if faculty have no role in determining students' grades. In fact, teachers make grading policy decisions that directly influence how students go about "earning" their grades. For example, faculty establish the cutoff levels between the grades. They decide whether extra credit is an option. The authors maintain it is more accurate to say that faculty "assign" grades based on what students "earned."

"The survey evidence from this study shows that there are widespread differences among economics instructors about what constitutes a grade in a principles of economics course." (p. 139) Some of the instructors grade using an absolute standard where the percentage of points needed for each grade is determined beforehand. Others grade on a curve or relative standard that depends on the performance in a particular course. The components used to determine grades—exams, quizzes, homework assignments, papers, or projects—were not the same. And even if there was some consistency, the various components were weighted differently. The exams themselves contained different kinds of questions, mostly fixed-response questions (multiple-choice, true-false), but also constructed-response questions and short and longer essay answers. Then these faculty reported a range of decisions as to whether course activities like participation were graded, whether missed exams could be made up, and whether grades close to the designated cutoff could, in some cases, be bumped up. We like to think our grading practices are objective, but policy decisions like these do add a certain subjectivity to the grade earning process.

Does diversity in grading matter? The question is whether this diversity matters. Does it make a difference? The way students shop around for courses—in some cases looking for what may look like easy courses and other times looking for features that fit with how they think a course should be—would indicate that these policy variations do make a difference for students. For them it is often about how they'll go about getting the grade, but for the rest of us the concern must also be about what and how students learn the content, and this is where the research lets us down. We don't know what combination of graded assignments promotes the most learning in which courses or for what students, for example. Most likely, there isn't a definitive answer to that question, but at this point we're making these policy decisions based on untested assumptions.

The authors provide one example of where diversity in grading practices is a problem. Researchers regularly examine the relationship between grades and any number of student variables, such as effort in courses, the selection of courses, gender differences in achievement, the willingness to take more courses in a discipline, or the student ratings of the course—the list is very long. In these studies, it is assumed that the letter grade given by one instructor is equivalent to the same grade given another instructor teaching a different section of the same course. In fact, "there may be subtle or substantial differences in how each professor grades that can affect the distribution of grades and the comparability of grades across instructors." (p. 346)

We aren't all operating from the same playbook when it comes to how grades are determined. What we have not done is consider the extent to which that's a problem regarding fairness and objectivity of the grades. We haven't linked our choices to learning. And we haven't spent much time thinking about how the diversity affects students who are already obsessively grade-oriented.

Reference

Walstad, W. B., and Miller, L. A., (2016). What's in a grade? Grading policies and practices in principles of economics. *Journal of Economic Education, 47* (4), 338–350.

Reprinted from *The Teaching Professor,* June 2017

Grading Advice: For Those Who Grade a Lot

Maryellen Weimer, PhD

Most teachers don't list grading as one of their favorite parts of teaching. If you're conscientious about it, it's a hard, time-consuming task. Dishearteningly, efforts to provide students with quality feedback aren't always appreciated, or at least they don't appear to be.

Any task that's done often tends to happen automatically, kind of like making the bed or taking the garbage out. For many teachers, there's less grading during the summer, which makes it a good time to reconsider ways to make this a manageable and meaningful task. This set of recommendations assumes you're grading papers of various sorts, products produced individually or in groups, and presentations. It's less about grading work with right answers, although some of the tenets of good grading practice apply across the board.

- Grading goes better if you **don't do it all at once**. If it's a task you don't like, it's easy to push it aside, which only makes it more unpleasant and easier still to put aside yet again. It's better to devote time to grading every day and then grade at a steady, rather than frenzied, pace, even if the paper stacks are multiple and tall. Take short breaks, let your mind wander, make tea, stretch, walk a bit, but don't get sidetracked answering email.

- **Try using a rubric**, if you don't already. They force teachers to think clearly about what they want to see in the assignment and that helps you stay objective and focused on the task when grading. Some faculty claim rubrics speed up the grading process, but that's only true if written comments are few. If distributed with the assignment, rubrics make it easier for students to understand the requirements. If the rubric is returned with the graded work, it can clarify the reasons for the grade.

- If you're providing handwritten feedback, remember: **if students can't read it, there's no reason to write it**. If you have papers that weren't picked up by the end of the year, give one to someone who doesn't know your handwriting well and ask him or her to read the comments.
- **Look at the language you're using**. A lot of terms widely used and understood by academics aren't familiar to students. It wouldn't hurt to make a list of your favorite feedback words and phrases and ask students to quickly define what those terms mean to them.
- **Offer more feedback during the process and less at the end**. If you point out problems and make suggestions for improvement before the final grade, students have a lot more reasons to act on the feedback. Moreover, having students submit work that's in progress teaches them something about partitioning tasks and helps with time management issues. It also makes grading at the end of the course more manageable: now you're only providing big-picture feedback.
- You can provide too much feedback, which teachers tend to do when the work submitted is poor. **Too much feedback overwhelms students** and often makes them feel they're so completely deficient, further effort is futile.
- **Always balance the feedback**. Find something positive to say even when most of the feedback deserves to be negative.
- With papers, products, and presentations, students (especially beginning ones) are terribly invested in what they've produced. The grade becomes an assessment of their inherent worth as persons. **Help students make the person–performance distinction**. The grade describes what they did, not what they can do.
- Many teachers now use elaborate, carefully calibrated point systems. These appear to make the grading process fair, objective, and precise. Point systems, in and of themselves, are none of these things. Grades are imprecise measures of learning and are easily manipulated by teachers. No teacher intends to be biased, but **teachers must work to be fair and objective**, something less easy to accomplish when grading tasks mount and tiredness descends.
- **If a student objects to a grade, don't say no immediately**. Rather, think of it as an opportunity for students to practice making a case in front of an authority. Listen to what they have to say. Ask questions. Further explain your justification. If they've made a valid point, adjust the grade.
- **We need to do our best with the grades**. They matter, often more than they should. Notably, they get students job interviews and into

grad school. They build confidence and diminish it. But in the larger scheme of life, grades don't matter. How long has it been since someone inquired about your GPA? In contrast, how long has it been since you made use of the skills and knowledge acquired in college?

Reprinted from *The Teaching Professor,* June 2016

Cumulative Tests and Finals

Maryellen Weimer, PhD

With the academic year nearly over and final exams upon us, it's a good time to consider how we assess student knowledge in our courses. Cumulative finals are still used in many courses, but a significant number of faculty have backed away from them because they are so unpopular with students, who strongly voice their preferences for exams that include only questions on content covered in that unit or module.

Although teachers should not ignore or discount student preferences across the board, there is the larger issue of which testing procedures best promote deep learning and lasting retention of course content. The evidence on the side of cumulative exams and finals is pretty much overwhelming, and those empirical results should not come as a surprise. An exam with questions on current and previous content encourages continued interaction with course material, and the more students deal with the content, the better the chances they will remember it. Students don't like cumulative exams for the very reason they ought to be used: preparing for them requires more time and energy devoted to understanding and remembering course content.

Cumulative finals are better than unit tests, but cumulative exams across the course are the best option if the goal is long-term retention. Good and plentiful research documents that students taking cumulative exams during the course score significantly higher when given content exams after the course is over.

The challenge is getting students on board with an exam procedure they don't like. That should start with a discussion of the rationale behind the teacher's decision to use cumulative exams, and it's a discussion that needs to occur early in the course. Part of what frightens students about cumulative tests is that studying for them seems overwhelming. The teacher can help here by exploring with them efficient ways to study sizable amounts of material—things such as regular, ongoing review (not just night-before-exam cramming) and study groups or even a single study buddy. Perhaps there's an extra-credit assignment (or regular credit assignment) that involves creating study questions or study guides, with the best ones posted on the course website or otherwise made available to the rest of the class.

Teachers can also help by regularly referencing content from previous units—asking questions about it, asking students to summarize key concepts that are relevant to material being covered now, challenging students to find things in their notes. Using content from different units helps construct that larger understanding of how all the course material relates and builds a coherent knowledge structure.

Incentives can encourage students to study hard and do well on cumulative finals. Other options might be used on cumulative tests with good performance on questions that cover previous content generating a bonus added to the exam score.

During the exam debrief, there might be a discussion of various strategies students are using to review previous material. Which ones are working; which ones are not? What new options might be tried for the next exam?

Students are never going to love exams. Most do understand that they are the way teachers discover what students know and justify the grades they earn. What more students need to understand is that certain kinds of exam experiences promote learning that lasts longer, which helps them in subsequent courses and after they graduate.

Here's a sample of the kind of research that documents the value of cumulative testing: Khanna, M. M., Badura Brack, A. S., & Finken, L. L. (2013). Short- and long-term effects of cumulative finals on student learning. *Teaching of Psychology, 40*(3), 175-182.

Reprinted from *The Teaching Professor,* May 2014

Learning about Learning after the Exam

Maryellen Weimer, PhD

Exam debriefs are typically that: brief. The tests are passed back, score ranges are revealed, and the teacher goes over the most missed questions, identifying and explaining the correct answer. There may be a chance for students to ask questions, but most sit passively. This way of debriefing exams is efficient but has little else going for it. Students miss questions in most cases because they don't know the material, which is the likely result of not having studied enough or not having used effective strategies when studying.

Favero and Hendricks observe, "Despite the fact that the cognitive tasks in college multiply and diversify, students generally apply their similar study techniques across multiple disciplines until those techniques no longer produce adequate results." (p. 325) They note that exam debriefs are a good time to confront study strategy issues. In two sections of a human anatomy course taken mostly by biology and nursing majors, students were invited to debrief their exam during the professor's office hours at any time before the second exam. Fifty-two percent of the students accepted the invitation, with the remaining students serving as a self-selecting control group.

The exam debriefing (ED) process consisted of four parts that the students completed before meeting with the professor. The authors shared the handout given to students:

- Part 1: Students looked carefully at the questions they missed and tried to determine why each question was missed.
- Part 2: Students then examined the questions to see if there was a pattern emerging. Did they miss questions for the same reason?
- Part 3: Students prepared a brief description of how they studied for the exam, including the amount of time devoted to studying.

- Part 4: Based on the information gleaned so far, students identified what changes they thought they could make that might help them better prepare for the next exam. They were given a list of areas where changes could be made: time on task, attending to detail, using active learning strategies, and general study habits. Examples were given in each of these areas.

After completing this ED analysis, students met briefly with the professor to discuss their "findings."

Favero states, "A significant difference was observed in the mean increase in exam performance from the first exam to the second exam for those students that conducted the ED. The calculated effect size was 0.48, demonstrating a moderate or medium effect size for the ED." (p. 324)

The most common reason by far for missing questions was simply not knowing the basic anatomical information needed to answer correctly or being able to narrow down the answer options but then choosing the wrong one. Interestingly but perhaps not surprisingly, the most common study strategies used were passive ones: reading the book, taking notes, and reviewing those materials. Only about 25 percent of students reported they discussed the material with others in the class, and less than 15 percent reported active strategies like taking online quizzes.

In the ED process students selected the behavior changes they believed they needed to make. All selected options from the active learning category in part, the authors believe, because those activities were demonstrated, modeled, and used in class. For example, many students reported using flashcards but only as devices that helped them memorize details like definitions. In class, Favero used an activity with flashcards that showed students how flashcards can be used more fruitfully to show relationships between, in this case, anatomical structure and function.

Did specific study behaviors account for the improvement in exam scores, or was it the result of participation in the whole process? The data collected here do not answer that question. It could be the more general approach of putting students in charge of a process through which they encountered themselves as learners who garnered these positive results. Whatever the cause, it's an interesting exploration of an approach that directly involves students in a debriefing process from which they stand to learn more about themselves as test takers.

Reference
Favero, T. G., & Hendricks, H. (2016). Student exam analysis (debriefing) promotes positive changes in exam preparation and learning. *Advances in Physiology Education, 40*(3), 323–328.

Note: Favero has also written an excellent article on in-class review sessions. Kudos to him for exploring instructional strategies that significantly bolster the learning potential of two class sessions that otherwise receive little attention in the literature.

Favero, T. G. (2011). Active review sessions can advance student learning. *Advances in Physiology Education, 35*(3), 247–248.

Reprinted from *The Teaching Professor,* November 2016

PART 4

•

Technology and Multimedia

Technology Policies: Are Some Better Than Others?

Maryellen Weimer, PhD

Students now arrive in our classrooms with a wide array of electronic devices. They also arrive used to being able to use those devices wherever and whenever they please. Should that include the classroom? The research is pretty conclusive that most students don't multitask well (certainly not as well as they think they do), and when they are attending to those devices they are not focusing on what's happening in class. But enforcing a ban on electronic devices can be difficult and time consuming, to say nothing of the adversarial relationship it cultivates between the teacher and students. Some teachers have decided that using the devices makes more sense than banning them. They have their students finding relevant information, locating answers, and even asking and responding to questions.

Faculty writing about technology policies usually recommend one or the other of these options: forbid the use of technology in the class or integrate it fully with course material. Generally, faculty opinions on the topic are strongly held. "What remains unclear is the extent to which such policies foster or undermine instructional outcomes." (p. 302) And that's the underlying question that has motivated several studies by Ledbetter and Finn, who report that their previous work "suggests that the relationship between teacher technology policies and instructional outcomes is complex and functions together with other instructor communication behaviors." (p. 302)

In this study, these researchers investigated the extent to which teacher technology policies predicted learner empowerment or "the student's motivation to achieve educational goals." (p. 302) They predicted that if the teacher's technology policies aligned with students' technology expectations, then learner empowerment would improve.

To address this and several other related hypotheses, the researchers looked at these two teacher policies—those that encouraged technology use and those that discouraged its use. They found that "students are most likely to feel that the course is valuable (meaningfulness) and that their participation makes a difference (impact) [both of these being established measures of empowerment] when the teacher highly encourages students to use technology for course-related purposes." (p. 312)

Another hypothesis proposed that if teachers moderately discouraged non-course-relevant use of technology that would also be associated with increased student empowerment. However, results here were opposite of what they predicted. Students were less empowered when the teacher moderately discouraged non-course-related technology usage than when the teacher either strongly discouraged or minimally discouraged its use.

They offer this implication of these results: "Although students may indeed prefer that instructors use a moderate level of technology, perhaps what is most important regarding technology policies is that the teacher has explicit rules regarding the use of technology in the classroom, clearly communicates the rules, and consistently enforces the rules." (p. 312)

This is a small study, and it addressed only one of many possible student outcomes. Nonetheless, it is interesting that discouraging the use of technology for non-course-related activities did not diminish how empowered these students felt about the course and their learning in it. Empowerment, or the motivation to learn, in this study suffered when teachers did not clearly either forbid it or permit it.

Reference

Ledbetter, A. M., & Finn, A. N. (2013). Teacher technology policies and online communication apprehension as predictors of learner empowerment. *Communication Education, 62*(3), 301-317.

Reprinted from *The Teaching Professor,* May 2014

Using Clickers Effectively: A Research-Based Tip

Maryellen Weimer, PhD

Use of clickers (or personal response systems, as they are officially known) continues to grow. They offer students a way to participate in large courses. They give faculty immediate feedback as to the level of understanding on a particular topic, concept, or issue. They add interest and variety to lectures. No wonder they have become so popular.

Clickers can be used in a variety of ways, but some common formats have emerged. For example, frequently, the question appears, students answer via their clickers, and the class responses are displayed. At that point, a discussion of the question and responses occurs, often between students sitting near each other. Students are then given a second opportunity to answer the question, after which the instructor shares the correct answer.

A group of biology faculty wondered if initially showing the class responses had any influence on student answers the second time they responded to the clicker question. To find out, they used a series of clicker questions in eight sections of an introductory biology course enrolling more than 600 students. In the control situation, students answered either a multiple-choice question or a true/false one, saw how the rest of the class responded, discussed the various options with their peers, and then re-answered the question. In the experimental situation, students answered the same two kinds of questions, but did not see how the class responded before they discussed the various answer options with their peers and then answered for a second time.

What happened? If students saw the bar graph indicating the class response to the question, they were 30 percent more likely to change from a less common response to the most common one. This trend was larger when the questions were true/false (38 percent changed to the common answer) than when the questions were multiple choice (28 percent changed to the common answer). The method used in the study allowed the researchers to determine that showing the bar graph biased the students. They changed their answers because they saw the class response, not because they were persuaded by the discussions held with their peers.

Bottom line based on these results: If you want students to talk about a question and their answers with peers and you want that discussion to influence whether or not students change their answers, do not show the class response before that peer discussion occurs.

Reference

Perez, K.E., Strauss, E.A., Downey, N., Galbraith, A., Jeanne, R., and Cooper, S. (2010). Does Displaying the Class Results Affect Student Discussion during Peer Instruction? *Cell Biology Education—Life Sciences Education,* 9, 133-140.

Reprinted from *The Teaching Professor,* March 2011

An Analysis of PowerPoint-Based Lectures

Maryellen Weimer, PhD

In many classrooms, PowerPoint slides have replaced the use of overhead projectors and the black (green or white) board. But despite their popularity, they aren't used by all instructors. In fact, in a recent study of business faculty members, almost 33 percent of the respondents said that they never used PowerPoint slides. Believe it or not, that was the most common response given. However, just over 40 percent of the respondents said that they always or frequently used PowerPoint.

The quantitative and qualitative analysis of PowerPoint use in business courses described in the article referenced below begins with an excellent review of the literature. The use of PowerPoint in college classrooms has been studied but with mixed results. PowerPoint does help structure content. It can offer visual representations of complex content; efficiently share diagrammatic information; and add interest with additions of clip art, color, and other design features. However, PowerPoint has been shown to make students more likely to skip class—this is true when the slides are available before/after class via some course management software. Students tend to take fewer notes when the slides are available. If students don't have access to the slides, they copy the slides verbatim without adding elaborations or putting ideas into their own words. Other studies have shown that students rely on the slides when they are preparing for exams. They spend more time with slides and less time actually reading their textbooks. Finally, some of the research is critical of the ways faculty use PowerPoint. One set of researchers cited in the article wrote that "PowerPoint presentations too often resemble a school play—very loud, very slow and very simple." (p. 247)

In this study, which included a survey of 230 business students in 14 different courses, the researchers found that student perceptions of the effectiveness of PowerPoint very much depended on the type of class. They rated its overall effectiveness highly in management courses and significantly lower in accounting courses. The researchers think that makes sense. PowerPoint is less adaptable to the demands of teaching quantitative content where teachers often model the problem-solving process.

In an interesting qualitative component of this research, another cohort of students was asked to share what they thought was good about faculty using PowerPoint in courses and what they thought was bad. The most frequently cited positive attributes were how PowerPoint can organize and structure course content and how it can add relevant graphs and other visual material. As for what these students thought was bad, the most common answer was the professor simply reading the slide word for word without translating, paraphrasing, or elaborating on the content. Interestingly, they also thought it was "bad" when the PowerPoints were available electronically, because then they had little motivation to take notes. Kudos to these students for recognizing the value of taking notes!

The article concludes with nine tips for using PowerPoint and making the slides an effective supplement to learning. Among that collection of tips are these:

- Carefully monitor how much information ends up getting included on the slide. The article's authors recommend no more than five bullet points. What's on the slide should serve to cue the instructor as to the next content that needs to be explained and elaborated.
- Don't go overboard with the number of slides. Too many can overwhelm students. "An instructor must have a good reason for showing each slide." (p. 250)
- "Do not let the PPT [PowerPoint] slides become the lecture. The slides should be an aid to the lecture but not the lecture itself." (p. 250)

Elsewhere in the article they caution against being "lured by irrelevant bells and whistles or gaudy color combinations for slide text and background." (p. 249) Too much clip art and animation and too many sound effects and cartoons distract students and compromise the potential of PowerPoint slides to promote learning.

Reference
Burke, L.A., James, K., and Ahmadi, M. (2009). Effectiveness of Power-Point-based lectures across different business disciplines: An investigation and implications. *Journal of Education for Business, 84* (4), 246-251.

Reprinted from *The Teaching Professor,* November 2009

PechaKucha and Ignite: Formats That Improve Student Presentations

Lynda Wolverton, Anna Butler, Carol Martinson, and Courtlann Thomas

Four of us who teach four separate courses (statistics, English, reading, and College Success) met to discuss student PowerPoint presentations and how they could be improved. Based on our experiences, we identified these common problems: slides overloaded with words and data; students who read their slides word for word; presentations that exceeded the allotted time; and uninteresting presentations that bored fellow classmates.

And it's not just students who exhibit these problems in their Power-Point presentations. In 2001, Angela R. Garber published an article that coined the now common phrase "Death by PowerPoint." Since then, numerous business professionals and educators have expanded the concept by writing books and articles and uploading video presentations that offer strategies and parodies to help everyone create savvier and more interesting PowerPoint presentations.

Based on our review of available options, we decided to see if we could help our students improve their presentations by having them use one of two related platforms, **PechaKucha** and **Ignite**. PechaKucha, which means "chitchat" in Japanese, is a PowerPoint format that was created by two architects, Astrid Klein and Mark Dythamin. It's a 20-slide, user-friendly, auto-timed slide show that allows the speaker 20 seconds per slide to speak. Sometimes PechaKucha is referred to as "20 x 20" or "6:40" as each presentation lasts exactly six minutes and 40 seconds. Ignite is a shortened version of PechaKucha launched in Seattle in 2006. Like PechaKucha, Ignite talks are auto-timed and use 20 slides but with only 15 seconds per slide, so they last a total of five minutes. These formats use pictures more often than words and sentences to illustrate the speaker's points. Other higher education faculty (in business and psychology, for example) have used PechaKucha and reported positive outcomes.

Each of us uploaded an auto-timed PechaKucha or Ignite template to our classes through the online supplemental space in the college's learning management system. After our students used them for their presentations, we compared experiences. Here's a list of the positive outcomes we experienced and then some notes about what we think will improve student presentations even further.

Positive outcomes:

1. There were no surprises. We knew exactly how much class time to allocate for presentations.
2. This presentation software gave us opportunities to reinforce information literacy concepts for citation and using graphics ethically.
3. The student presentations celebrated individuality; students who had similar topics created very different presentations.
4. Each of us found it easy to develop rubrics that helped students meet the objectives of the assignments. Students knew exactly what was expected and how their presentations would be graded.
5. The software worked well in an online environment. The newest PowerPoint software allows students to record audio as they present the slides.
6. The format encouraged deep learning, scaffolding, and critical thinking. Students need to have a thorough understanding of their topic and the points they want to make in a time-sensitive environment.
7. By linking the auto-timed templates to the online learning management system course shells, collateral learning took place for first-time-in-college students and students who had never taken an online course, by introducing them to successful navigation in the learning management system.

What we'll do differently the next time we use these presentation formats:

1. Reinforce the differences between a traditional PowerPoint and PechaKucha and Ignite.
2. Reinforce the importance of practicing prior to the class presentation. Twenty seconds is a long time if a student has only a word or two to say per slide. On the other hand, time slips away quickly if a student has quite a bit to say per slide. In fact, one of us has decided to use the Ignite format next term because the PechaKucha slide discussions were too long.

3. Emphasize the importance of using pictures. Some students still created a traditional PowerPoint presentation with words (and few pictures) and read through each slide quickly in concert with the timed presentation.

4. Encourage students to use note cards. Even if they had practiced, they sometimes forgot their content when they were in front of an audience.

5. Encourage students to use their own photos or those from open share photo sites such as Flickr, morgueFile, and Coppermine, to name a few.

6. After each presentation, allow follow-up questions.

Overall, all four of us agreed that using both PechaKucha and Ignite were preferable alternatives to traditional PowerPoint for student presentations in our courses.

Reprinted from *The Teaching Professor,* May 2014

What Research Tells Us about Online Discussion

John Orlando, PhD

Student discussion differentiates online education from the old correspondence courses. But there are still many questions to answer in order to facilitate good discussion online. Hong Zhiu, of the University of Texas at San Antonio, did a meta-analysis of studies of online discussion over the past 15 years and has interesting findings about participation. These findings can help instructors maximize the benefits of discussion.

A few students dominate. Studies show that a few students tend to dominate discussion, just as a few people tend to dominate face-to-face discussions. Yet, most students still talk more in an online discussion than in a face-to-face environment, lending evidence to the perception that online education tends to draw shy students out of their shells. This is one major advantage of online education, and a reason why discussion should be central to any online course.

The finding also reminds us that even in an online discussion, equal participation is not likely. While it is important to establish minimum requirements for participation, human nature means that some students will still dominate. In fact, trying to even out participation rates might have undesirable consequences. Requiring too many discussion posts from each student will lead to students posting just to meet the guidelines.

While we want students to learn how to express themselves, we might also consider the legitimate role of a "passive participant." Maybe that person is a good listener, while another who contributes a lot is a poor listener. The online instructor should ask whether the purpose of discussion is to get everyone to talk or to generate good ideas. If the latter, then craft discussion requirements to allow for discussion supporters who encourage others but do not take a larger role.

Participation between students increases over time. Studies have
shown that initial discussion tends to be between faculty and students, but
as time goes on, students start talking to one another more and more. This
is encouraging, and the goal of an online course is to move the center of
gravity of a class from the lecture to the discussion. The design of a traditional classroom with desks facing the instructor embodies the assumption
that students are there to listen, and as a result discussion goes through the
instructor. But everyone is in an equal position in an online discussion, so
students tend to start genuinely speaking to one another.

This does not mean that online instructors should remove themselves
entirely from discussion. Students want the instructor to be present, at the
very least to demonstrate that students' points are valued. A good guideline
is that an online instructor should foster, but not dominate, discussion. Provide the structure and initial nudge, but hope that it eventually gets taken
over by students.

Constructive interactions. A third theme is that the majority of discussion is collaborative and constructive. Researchers found that responses
generally contained supportive messages about others' postings. This is important, as people who do not teach online often assume that students will
start flaming on online discussion boards. Flaming is context-dependent.
Unlike in other forums, online students are not truly anonymous, and because the instructor holds the grades there is a built-in deterrent to flaming.
Studies also show that responses to others were far more common in discussions than original postings. This again makes sense, as any discussion
generally starts with an initial topic and then builds on that.

But the finding draws into question the common requirement in online
courses that all students make an original posting. This can create multiple
discussion threads that are hard to follow. Students will also run out of original ideas after a few postings are made and turn their "original" postings
into unoriginal comments.

Consider the purpose of the original posting requirement. It is to generate creativity? If so, then a response to someone else's point might contain
more insight and creativity than an original posting. Maybe instead of requiring an original posting and one or two replies to others, just require one
or two original thoughts.

The fact that most responses were supportive also raises the question
of whether students are too nice in discussion. Some studies suggest that
students are unwilling to challenge one another in discussion. Has the focus
on acceptance and inclusion in today's education landscape led students to
be hesitant to disagree? The purpose of academic discussion is to model civil

and constructive disagreement as a means of intellectual progress, and so an online instructor might deliberately "stir the pot" with postings that invite disagreement as a way to facilitate robust interaction and engagement.

Reference
Zhou, H. (2015). A Systematic Review of Empirical Studies on Participants' Interactions in Internet- Mediated Discussion Boards as a Course Component in Formal Higher Education Settings, *Online Learning Journal,* v. 19, n. 3.

Reprinted from *Online Classroom,* February 2016

Are the Videos in Your Courses Promoting Learning?

Maryellen Weimer, PhD

Video material is now an important instructional component of face-to-face, blended, and online courses. Research supports its potential to promote learning, but those benefits aren't automatic—it's not just the video, but how that video material is designed and integrated into the course. Selecting the videos is important, but how they are used in large measure determines the extent to which they enhance learning.

"What, then, are the principles that allow instructors to choose or develop videos that are effective in moving students toward the desired learning outcomes?" (p. 1) That's the question Cynthia Brame addresses. She explores three principles with "elements [that] provide a solid base for the development and use of video as an effective educational tool." (p. 1)

Cognitive Load: This cognitive psychology theory suggests that memory has several interconnected components. It starts with sensory memory, which is the extrapolation of information from the environment. That information goes into working (or short-term) memory, which has a limited capacity. The information in working memory must be encoded before it can be transferred to long-term memory. Because working memory has limited capacity, the learner must be selective about what goes into it. Cognitive load theory proposes that those selections are based on the *intrinsic load* or perceived interest, importance, and relevance of the information. Selections are also influenced by *germane load*, which is the level of cognitive activity required—more bluntly, how much work is involved in understanding the content and connecting it with what is already known. Finally, what each learner decides to place in working memory can be influenced by *extraneous load*—what's being delivered that gets in the way of learning, like confusing instructions or extraneous information.

When the material is being conveyed via video, still more factors come into play. The information can be delivered visually or it can be auditory, or it can be communicated by both simultaneously. Information can be processed by both, but either channel can overwhelm the other.

If the goal is making videos that minimize extraneous cognitive load and optimize germane load, cognitive *signaling* or cueing can help. It directs attention to on-screen text or symbols that highlight important information. For example, if the color changes or a symbol draws attention to a particular part of the screen, this helps students keep track of what's important. *Segmenting* the material in videos allows those viewing the video to deal with small chunks of new content. YouTube Annotate and HapYak can be used to give learners control over the flow of information. They enable those watching to pause the video. *Weeding* involves the elimination of interesting but nonessential information. A video with music, complex backgrounds, and extra animation increases extraneous load and may mean the learner is missing the most important material. Finally, video material should *match modality* to the content. If the content involves a complex process that can be explained by a talking head, that explanation will be enhanced if it's accompanied with complementary visual material, such as diagrams, sketches, or pictures.

Student Engagement: This principle is more widely understood than cognitive load. "The idea is simple: If students do not watch the video, they cannot learn from them." (p. 3) And the best advice here is equally simple: keep it short. Brame highlights research on 6.9 million video-watching sessions by students in massive open online courses (MOOCs). If the video was less than six minutes long, the median engagement time was almost 100 percent, but it dropped to 50 percent when the video was nine to 12 minutes and 20 percent for 12 to 40-minute videos. How the content is delivered in the video also impacts engagement. It's higher when the style is conversational and delivered with enthusiasm.

Active Learning: Watching a video is a passive activity unless it has design features that promote involvement. Technology now makes it possible to add questions within the video. Research shows that students who watched videos with interpolated questions did better on exams than students who watched videos without them. Even a set of guiding questions that students consider as they watch the video had positive effects on test performance. Further, videos can be made so that students can control how they're used. They can move back to listen again to something they might not have understood, or they can review certain segments they deem especially important. Finally, Brame suggests making the video part of a larger homework assignment.

Reference
Brame, C. J., (2016). Effective educational videos: Principles and guidelines for maximizing student learning from video content. *Cell Biology Education—Life Sciences Education, 15* (4), 1–6.

Reprinted from *The Teaching Professor,* January 2017

Have You Considered Using Open Textbooks?

John Hilton III and Kenneth L. Alford

College textbooks are expensive, and prices continue to rise. The Bureau of Labor reported a 600 percent increase in textbook costs between 1980 and 2012[1]. The average 2015 American college student graduated with over $35,000 of student debt, a portion of which came from textbook costs[2]. In a recent survey of over 22,000 college students, 64 percent reported not purchasing a required textbook because it was too expensive, 49 percent stated that textbook costs caused them to take fewer courses, and 34 percent declared they had earned a poor grade in one or more courses because they could not afford to buy the textbook[3].

Students cope with this problem in a variety of ways—purchasing older editions of textbooks, delaying their purchases, sharing textbooks with other students, or avoiding textbook purchases altogether. What can be done to alleviate this problem?

One promising solution is open textbooks, part of a larger Open Educational Resources (OER) initiative[4]. OER typically use Creative Commons licenses that provide professors and students with more permissions than traditional copyrights do, such as granting permission to edit or delete text[5]. OER have been used in hundreds of colleges and universities throughout the United States and Canada, including Harvard University, University of Illinois (Urbana-Champaign), Purdue University, Brigham Young University, University of British Columbia, and the University of Calgary[6].

Advantages

- **Inexpensive.** One obvious advantage of open textbooks is that they are free. Digital copies can be accessed online; printed versions can be made available at a cost. Whether choosing texts in print or digital format, students save money in courses that adopt an open textbook.

- **Adaptable.** A second advantage is that open textbooks easily support reuse and revision[7]. They can be customized to match your course by adding, removing, reordering, or modifying content. You can even combine content from two or more open texts to create a new book. For example, a colleague of ours who teaches nonnative English-speaking students adapted open psychology textbooks to create a text appropriate for his students' language skills. Additionally, some professors have observed that adopting an open textbook provided them with an opportunity and incentive to look at their courses anew, improving them.
- **Portable.** Electronic open textbooks can be accessed by students on essentially any computer, tablet, or smartphone platform. While not all students will want to read textbooks digitally, it has been our experience that a majority of students are happy to read textbooks on their devices—especially if those textbooks are free.
- **Timely.** Standard textbooks in many disciplines tend to lag behind the state of the art because they are slow and expensive to produce. Open textbooks, on the other hand, can be updated quickly. If you find information that is out of date, you can update it and provide the corrected text to your students.

Concerns

- **Quality.** If the old adage "You get what you pay for" is true, then some might ask, "If open textbooks are free, how can they be any good?" A review of nine recent studies regarding the use of open educational resources concluded that using OER does not appear to decrease student learning. Roughly half of the almost 5,000 students and teachers surveyed found OER to be comparable to traditional resources. Approximately 35 percent believed they were superior, and only 15 percent found them to be inferior[8].
- **Availability.** The question quickly arises: "Is there an existing open textbook appropriate for my course?" Hundreds of open textbooks exist. It is true, though, that they are more likely to be available for introductory courses than for specialized and upper-division courses.
- **Convenience.** Like everything else associated with teaching, there are trade-offs involved with using open textbooks. Recognize that it will take time to identify suitable texts and reject others that do not meet your needs. It will also take time to adjust your syllabi, slideshows, assignments, and assessments to closely align with any new textbook.

Getting Started

After you decide to consider the possibility of switching to an open textbook, how can you find and survey your available options? One resource is the University of Minnesota's Open Textbook Library (http://open.umn.edu/opentextbooks/), a repository of open textbooks that also includes faculty textbook reviews. Numerous other repositories are also available[9]. Using these, you can find, download, and evaluate potential open textbooks as desired.

If a quality open textbook alternative is available, the decision to switch can provide immediate financial benefits to your students and result in a textbook you are able to tailor to your students' needs. You will never know what is available until you investigate for yourself. Based on our experience, we recommend that you give it a try!

Notes

1 Bureau of Labor Statistics. *http://www.bls.gov/cpi/*.

2 *http://blogs.wsj.com/economics/2015/05/08/congratulations-class-of-2015-youre-the-most-indebted-ever-for-now/*.

3 Florida Virtual Campus (2012). Florida Student Textbook Survey. Tallahassee. *http://www.openaccesstextbooks.org/pdf/2012_Florida_Student_Textbook_Survey.pdf*.

4 For additional information on OER, see *https://library.educause.edu/resources/2010/5/7-things-you-should-know-about-open-educational-resources*.

5 For additional information on Creative Commons, see *https://creativecommons.org/licenses/*.

6 A list of colleges that have adopted open textbooks published by Rice University is provided at *https://openstax.org/adopters*. Note that these textbooks are only a small fraction of the total number of open textbooks that are currently available.

7 Bissell, Ahrash N. Permission granted: Open licensing for educational resources. *Open Learning*, 24 (1) (February 2009), 97–106.

8 Hilton III, J. Open educational resources and college textbook choices: A review of research on efficacy and perceptions. *Educational Technology Research and Development*. (Forthcoming.)

9 See also the California Open Online Library for Education (*http://coolfored.org/*) and the repository finder hosted by BC Campus in Vancouver, British Columbia: *https://open.bccampus.ca/open-textbook-101/where-to-find-open-textbooks/*.

Reprinted from *The Teaching Professor,* August 2016

Digital Content Curation

Lisa M. Shappee

We run across excellent online content all the time. Instructional designers are always finding new tools and applications that would be of interest to faculty and course designers. Librarians also frequently have a wealth of information on systems that would benefit those involved in developing and teaching online courses. Plus, every member of a department encounters tools that others would find helpful in teaching their courses and material in their subject that would interest their colleagues and help students research topics for class.

But most people keep this content to themselves. Digital content repositories are a great way to share your finds with others. Below are two good tools for curating digital content online. These tools were chosen because they are available on multiple platforms, including Apple iOS and Android. They also allow collaboration. You can invite contributors, allow departments to work together, or perhaps utilize them for group projects for students. Both of these tools have browser buttons for utilization when on the Web as well. If a contributor finds content of interest, he or she simply clicks the browser button and the content will be shared automatically, allowing quicker and easier content curation. These tools do more than just provide a list of links; they also make the content more graphical, allowing users to decide what they want to read based on visuals rather than just words.

Flipboard (*https://flipboard.com*) is touted as a digital personalized news magazine that allows you to create a magazine not only for your own personal use but also for curating content for others. Flipboard only allows the curation of online content such as articles, blog posts, and tweets, making it a great choice for curating content on current issues. As you add new content, Flipboard reorganizes the information with the most recent content first, but it does allow editing that lets you organize or even delete articles as needed. Flipboard's visually appealing style of presentation and organization gives users a new look and feel that might be different from a generic list of links or a wiki. When used on a computer, Flipboard is displayed like a blog, but on a mobile device the user is able to swipe pages as if reading a digital magazine. This trendier and techie look may make the users more likely to scroll through and read more content and even have them coming back for more as you add more pertinent content. Follow this link to see an example of a Flipboard magazine on educational technology: *http://flip.it/Vd4bv.*

Flipboard is also great for personal use. Users can add their own social media accounts to their Flipboard magazine, turning their Facebook and Twitter accounts into a visually appealing digital magazine. This tool also allows you to search by topic and find other content feeds to follow, allowing you to completely customize your experience. This type of customization can also lead to easier content curation, as you can choose to share any information you find in your own Flipboard magazine or on other social media platforms.

Pearltrees (*www.pearltrees.com*) is different from Flipboard in that you can share many different types of information. This tool allows you to share Web pages, photos, PDFs, PowerPoints, and much more. One great perk of this tool is that when you share content like file attachments, the user can view the content in Pearltrees. There is no need to open another program or window. Since Pearltrees allows the attaching of files, it is not only useful for content curation but can also be utilized for group projects. Pearltrees also allows notes, which allows users to type notes or information within their Pearltrees bundles to help explain something or to give direction to group members for next steps in the project.

Pearltrees organizes information in bundles, or trees, that can branch out into other areas. For example, a Pearltree about iPad apps can have multiple bundles under it, like productivity and weather apps; see the example found at *http://tinyurl.com/oglkuzo.* This tool allows you to search other users' trees by topic and then subscribe to them or add the content to your own collection. As you continue to follow others and curate your own content, the bundles become interconnected, allowing a community of content curators to share content on similar interests. In effect, other Pearltrees users are helping you curate content as they add to their own collections to which you subscribe.

Anyone can be a curator by helping students, colleagues, and even one's self find the right information on just the right topic.

Reprinted from *Online Classroom,* April 2016

Creating Accessible Video for the Online Classroom

Krisa Greear and Patrick R. Lowenthal

Videos are being integrated more and more into the online classroom. However, they can create barriers for learners with hearing problems. If a student asks for an ADA accommodation for a video, you will be scrambling at the last minute to create a text supplement. That's why it's good practice to create a text supplement at the same time that you create a video.

Many faculty use separate transcripts to add text for hearing-impaired students. But this makes it challenging for a deaf or hard-of-hearing student to absorb the visual and auditory information simultaneously, as they need to shift back and forth between the images and text. The better way to create accessible video is with captions that appear within the video itself, allowing learners to read the text with the images. While captioning takes time, the steps are not difficult to master, and there are a variety of options for adding captions to online videos.

A common way to caption videos is to do it yourself, either in two steps, creating the transcript and then adding it to the video, or in one step with software that creates the captions automatically from the video. While the former process sounds more time-consuming, automated systems often make a lot of mistakes and require editing the results later on. This is why some people prefer making the transcript manually. Below is a description of each process.

Two-step process
   Step one: Create the transcript
   • **Manual creation:** Type a script before you create the video and then read from it when recording your video narration. This option can work well, but it can be very challenging for faculty using video in a less scripted manner (e.g., instructional screencasts of software).

- **Desktop software:** Speak into speech-to-text software like Dragon NaturallySpeaking for PC to translate your words into written text. The quality has come a long way from the early days of speech recognition, but the results will still need to be edited for errors.
Step two: Sync the transcript to video
- **Web-based software:** Upload your video to YouTube and then upload the transcript file afterwards. The system will read the transcript and sync the two by determining when the text needs to appear on the screen.
- **Commercial provider:** You can pay a commercial provider a fee to take your video and transcript and sync the two. These providers use human or computer efforts to ensure the captions show at the appropriate time.

One-step process

Another option is to use software that creates captions right off the audio in the video, thus avoiding the two-step process outlined above. However, the features, methodology, and capabilities of each software program vary widely.

- **Web-based software:** YouTube is a popular video application that has built-in speech recognition to create automated captions. Again, the results will need to be edited for accuracy.
- **Desktop software:** Some lecture-capture or presentation-creation software have a built-in captioning feature. Captivate allows you to (a) create a presentation, create a transcript separately, and then sync the words with the video to create captions or (b) create a presentation, export audio, submit audio to a vendor for captioning with speech-to-text software to have the computer create a transcript, then sync the words with the video to create captions. Camtasia Studio is another popular option. You can add captions manually with Camtasia Studio or use its speech-to-text tool to create the transcript. (Please note the captioning feature is currently available only for the PC version; the Mac version of Camtasia does not have this capability.) In our experience, some faculty find using Camtasia Studio easier than others do.

Pay for it: Commercial providers

Given the time it takes to create captions yourself, many colleges and universities use commercial providers to caption online-course videos. Commercial providers can (a) create or edit a transcript only, (b) sync or merge the transcript to a video, or (c) create an interactive transcript that is search-able by word. Some providers can also translate videos and even add captions to videos that you didn't create and do not own. Rev.com is a popular option. Receive captions in 24 to 48 hours for as little as $1 a minute.

Pay for it: Freelancers

One last option is to pay a freelancer to create a transcript for you. Fiverr.com lists dozens of freelancers who will caption 15 minutes of video for $5 (often more for multiple speakers or quick turnaround). If you have flexibility, freelancers might be the cheapest way to get a transcript created, and therefore, extremely useful if you are paying for these services out of your own pocket.

Additional resources:

Still looking for more support? Check out these two websites:
• University of Washington: Caption your own video for free
http://www.washington.edu/accessibility/videos/free-captioning/
This website covers topics including captioning your own video for free, how to add caption files to video, adding captions to YouTube videos, and adding captions to videos on web pages.
• DCMP: Caption it yourself
https://www.dcmp.org/ciy/
This website includes sections on: Web-Based Captioning/Subtitling Tools, Desktop Captioning/Subtitling Software, Caption-Ready Video Hosting Providers, How to Caption It Yourself, and Guidelines for Captions.

Video captioning is not difficult and is a critical component for creating an accessible online course.

Reprinted from *Online Classroom,* January 2016

PART 5
•
Special Considerations

'100 Things Restaurant Staffers Should Never Do': Adapted for Teachers

Grace Johnson

On October 29 and November 5, 2009, *The New York Times*' Small Business blog ran two parts of a posting titled "100 Things Restaurant Staffers Should Never Do." As I read the list, it occurred to me that some of author Bruce Buschel's ideas might be applicable (with minor alterations) to teachers. As we begin winter terms and spring semesters, here are 10 items from that list that I think could help us create classrooms that are even more conducive to learning.

#1—Do not let anyone enter the restaurant without a warm greeting. Do not let anyone enter your classroom without a warm greeting. Smile, face your students, and make them feel welcome.

#9—Do not recite the specials too fast or robotically or dramatically. You aren't delivering a soliloquy or auditioning for a part. Do not lecture too fast or robotically or dramatically. Teachers shouldn't be delivering soliloquies. They aren't auditioning. We are talking to students who are hearing the topic for the first time (OK, maybe the second time for those students repeating your class). Although we have delivered this lecture once or twice each semester for the last 19 years, it needs to be as fresh and interesting as it was the first time we presented it.

#15—Never say "I don't know" to any question without following with, "I'll find out." Great advice for teachers! Do you know everything about your discipline? An inquisitive student's curiosity should not be turned off by a teacher who dismisses or avoids questions to which answers are not handily available.

#46—Never acknowledge any one guest over and above any other. All guests are equal. Students are also equal and should not be acknowledged preferentially. It's satisfying and easy to interact with academically talented students or those with whom we share a common interest (e.g., living/working abroad experiences, research interests, musical tastes, or sports teams). But all students deserve our attention and the opportunity to interact with us.

#47—Do not gossip about co-workers or guests within earshot of guests. Do not gossip about colleagues or students when other students can hear you. Complaints, questions, or general observations about students, grades, your department, your colleagues, or the institution are better left unsaid when students are anywhere around.

#50—Do not turn on the charm when it's tip time. Be consistent throughout. Do not turn on the charm when it's course evaluation time. Your behavior should be consistent across the course.

#63—Never blame the chef, the busboy, the hostess, or the weather for anything that goes wrong. Just make it right. Never blame the registrar's office, the information technology office, the bookstore, or the department staff assistant for anything that goes wrong. Just make it right. Take the needed time to resolve problems or direct students to the person with the power to fix what has gone wrong.

#70—Never deliver a hot plate without warning the guest. And never ask a guest to pass that hot plate down the table. Never deliver surprises to students. Don't change important assignments or their due dates unless you must. Then give students plenty of warning about the change. Don't suddenly spring new assignments or expectations on students without first giving plenty of advance notice.

#77—Do not disappear. Be available for your students, your colleagues, your admissions office, or your undergraduate research office. Balancing the demands of research and scholarship, service to the institution, and teaching is difficult for all of us. Fortunately, various information technologies make it easy for us to stay in contact with and be available to students.

#99—Do not show frustration. Your only mission is to serve. Be patient. It is not easy. Students (like customers) can be terribly frustrating, but we should work not to show that frustration. We are guides and mentors. Teaching takes patience, and some days it isn't always easy to find, but we still have a responsibility to look for it.

Buschel's complete list might delight, amuse, annoy, frustrate, or insult you. I'm hoping that these adaptations will encourage you to reflect on how students are treated in your classroom. New terms and semesters are great times to begin anew. We need to make sure that the ways we treat students reflect the highest professional standards. That way we know we've done our part to make their learning experiences rich and satisfying.

Reprinted from *The Teaching Professor,* January 2010

Psychological Perspectives on Managing Classroom Conflict

Jim Guinee

For the past 10 years, I've given a presentation on managing classroom conflict to new faculty at my institution. I'm a psychologist, so that's the unique perspective I offer. Throughout the presentation I emphasize the need to analyze "cognitive errors," which I define as the faulty assumptions or misinterpretations commonly made by new (and not so new) faculty. These ways of responding to negative student behavior are ineffective; sometimes they even make it worse. I'd like to highlight several of these.

Most new faculty want to come across as being nice. When negative behaviors surface, they secretly hope they will disappear, particularly due to the mistaken belief that being nice and being respected always go hand in hand. Unfortunately, generally the negative behavior not only doesn't disappear, it gets transmitted to other students like a virus.

Then there's the error I call the "misperception of colleague individuality." Each class, each teacher, has a different set of rules. For example, some instructors ban laptops from the classroom, while others require students to sit in the front row and still others do not allow makeups under any circumstances. Then there are those teachers who don't specify any policies either verbally or in writing. For students who encounter a different set of rules in every class, it's confusing. That's why I advise new (and experienced) instructors to be very explicit in the syllabus regarding classroom rules and consequences (e.g., cell phones, leaving class early).

Finally, new instructors tend to personalize negative behavior from students. For example, a student may be taking 15 hours and working full-time to pay the bills. Is it any surprise that this student dozes off during an afternoon class? How should an instructor interpret this behavior? That's an important question because how a teacher reacts depends on how he or she has interpreted the behavior. In this case I'd say you might want to give the student the benefit of the doubt. Don't immediately see this as a student problem. You may still need to wake up the student, but that's not because you put him or her to sleep.

I also offer new instructors a variety of helpful suggestions, many focused on the relationship that exists between teacher and student and the behavioral responses that are important in most interpersonal relationships. For example, I recommend specifically disclosing to another person your "issues" or "pet peeves." On the first day of class I share with students something I call "10 simple rules for taking my class." One of the rules is titled "Stay seated unless you see smoke." No doubt every instructor has encountered students who for various reasons feel it necessary to begin packing up before class is dismissed. Early on in my teaching career I realized not only that I found it distracting, but it made me ANGRY. Therefore, I do what we call in counseling "owning" the problem. I acknowledge to the students that it is something that bothers ME; therefore, it is MY problem. Amazingly this proves to be very effective and almost completely eliminates the behavior from ever occurring.

Although we've been discussing common behavior problems, students are not always in complete control of their behavior. Some negative student behavior is the result of psychological problems. My experience with new faculty is that they are often compassionate and want to help, but they are afraid they might offend the student. They also feel a bit reluctant to discuss personal issues with students. On my campus, we have a link on our website specifically for assisting faculty with counseling center referrals [*www.uca.edu/counseling/howtomakeareferral.php*]. We encourage faculty to call and discuss observations, and we suggest strategies for responding to a troubled student.

In conclusion, I recommend improving classroom management by examining the individual you are in control of—yourself. By looking at such areas as distorted thinking, disclosure to students, and behavioral changes, you can effect much positive change in the classroom and do so without even getting involved with students over the behavior issues.

Reprinted from *The Teaching Professor,* October 2009

The Day I Walked out of My Classroom

Mary J. DeYoung

We teachers often comment about how we learn so much from our students. It's part cliché, part personal modesty, and part true. Usually, I learn some detail of a particular math problem when a student sees a relationship or pattern that I had never noticed. Occasionally, a student presents a new way to solve a problem. But what I'd like to write about here is the day students forced a 180-degree shift in my thinking about classroom discourse.

"Jigsaw Jorge" was the day's problem, and this was a math course for pre-service elementary teachers. We'd been together as a class for six months. They knew my questioning style and our classroom pattern of group work followed by whole-class debriefing. As we discussed Jorge and their solution ideas, the answers fell into two very different camps. Some groups had added the relevant numbers, while others had multiplied those same numbers, with very different results. This was not a problem with multiple solutions, so we were committed to reaching consensus.

That's when it happened. I decided to make them sort it out on their own. I announced that I was leaving to take a lap around the building so that they could settle the debate themselves. After my first loop, I made several passes by the classroom. Each time, those near the door gave me a "keep walking" signal. I complied, finally returning when 10 minutes of the period remained. At that point, the class was conducting a final, nearly unanimous vote. They shared their conclusion and we celebrated their good work.

The following day, we discussed the method. As teachers, they will make many mathematical decisions on their own. I wanted them to see how classroom teachers might act when caught in a "which is right" dilemma. I wanted them to spar with each other over their rationales and through that process see how they might use their future teacher colleagues.

147 |

Because I missed out on the nitty-gritty of their discussions, I invited them to reflect via email. They indicated that my leaving them alone had been a good learning experience. They described initially "just looking at each other" before moving into "back-and-forth discussions" that led to campaigning for their positions, and the series of votes.

But it was the following email from which I learned the most:

While you were out of the classroom, I believe that class felt a weight off their shoulders. Not because you are a mean person by any means, but because they felt more free to say things they would not say when you are around. I think this is because you have the answer and can tell us if we are wrong or right and point us in the right direction, so maybe some people get embarrassed by that. When you were out of the classroom no one really knew the answer and everyone was throwing out ideas and speaking more freely. They were not afraid of getting embarrassed because no one knew the answer.

Did you catch what that student wrote? I was a "weight on their shoulders"? Wow—that hit me between the eyes!

As a veteran mathematics teacher, I see abundant math anxiety and even outright hatred for the subject. Students exhibit different levels of comfort about speaking up in class. But I had always perceived that it was about the other students. I believed they were reluctant to ask stupid questions in front of their peers. But in fact it was me. They did not want to look stupid in front of me. How could it take 30 years to realize this simple fact?

In discussing this experience, a colleague wisely observed how we always interpret our interactions with others through our own lens. I was projecting onto the students my own thinking about our working relationship. I see myself as their academic stimulus—their helper and travel guide into the subject of mathematics. They see me as a taskmaster (albeit a benevolent one, or at least "not mean"), and as judge and jury. These students view me in a completely different way than I expected. They know that I'm holding their future grade and they never really forget that.

How is this new mind-set affecting my teaching? I'm approaching my classroom and office interactions with students in a new way, listening more and talking less. I am more cognizant of the great divide created by the ever-present power differential. I'm working harder to meet my students in the middle of that divide.

Reprinted from *The Teaching Professor*, November 2008

What Do I Need to Know About and Do for Students with Learning Disabilities?

Karen Eifler and Melanie Gangle

At the beginning of each semester, among the flurry of papers flooding my mailbox are a handful of accommodation plans for students in my classes who have learning disabilities. Some of them must have exams *read* to them. Some must have *extra time* provided for exams. Some need handouts to be printed in 28-point font. Whatever happened to "I teach, they learn, I test, and they tell me what they've learned"? I confess to some crankiness. Are all these accommodations really necessary? I decided I would call Melanie, the coordinator of our Office for Students with Disabilities. The conversation was enlightening, and I thought I would share some of it with you.

Karen: *What is the point of these accommodation plans your office sends me each semester?*

Melanie: Thank you for caring enough about your students to call! An accommodation plan for students with disabilities specifies the "academic adjustments and auxiliary aids" (Section 504 of the Rehabilitation Act of 1973) and/or "program modifications" (Title II of the Americans with Disabilities Act) that each student needs in order to learn, take exams, and participate in campus activities. You play a vital role in ensuring that our institution complies with the law, by providing these accommodations in your courses and working with my office to ensure that each student receives appropriate accommodations.

Karen: *What about those students who come up to me on the day of an exam, or maybe the day before, and simply announce that they are entitled to extra time because they have a learning disability? Their names aren't on any list you've provided. Am I obligated to provide them accommodations?*

Melanie: Each institution may have a slightly different system, so I recommend that faculty contact their local disability services office for clarification about policies. In general, if a student does not have an accommodation plan in place, you may provide exam accommodations but are not required to do so. However, I think students benefit when they don't have to rush to complete exams. Many students without disabilities need more time on exams, such as ESL students, students with temporary illness, or those distracted by a difficult family situation, for example. And all students benefit when there is time to check their work. **Karen:** *Some of these accommodations make me feel as though I'm enabling bad habits, especially if other students aren't getting extra time and start complaining that it isn't fair. How do you recommend I respond to complaints from other students?*

Melanie: You must protect the confidentiality of students with disabilities, although tension always exists between providing accommodations and ensuring confidentiality. If you hear another student complaining about exam accommodations, the best response is that everyone has unique circumstances. In advance of complaints, it helps to review your policies with the class on the first day and as exams get closer. Explain your course expectations and offer to discuss individual student concerns or requests for extensions on a case-by-case basis. For example, you probably allow time extensions for other reasons also, such as a death in the family or illness.

Karen: *A lot of this just seems like extra work to me. Do I really have to prepare separate sets of materials for students or record reading materials for students with visual impairments?*

Melanie: You don't have to do these things yourself. Our office can assist you in preparing alternate electronic, large-print, or Braille formats for students with visual impairments. When planning your courses, prepare your handouts and readings in accessible formats, even if you don't have a specific student who needs alternate materials right now. Another great idea: some faculty record their lectures as podcasts to allow students to listen to lectures at home while studying.

Karen: *What if I make all these accommodations and the student still does poorly? Am I liable in any way? Even if students have a learning disability, they are, after all, adults and in college. Shouldn't they be managing their own learning?*

Melanie: It is indeed *the student's responsibility* to advocate for his or her own learning needs and to work with you for support. If you have a student with a disability who is not doing well in your course, I recommend that you follow your usual protocol—if you offer warnings, you can also refer that student to my office for help. Each student should be assessed on the standards you have set for your course, whether they have a disability or not. It does not benefit any student to receive a grade that he or she has not earned.

Karen: *One last question: it seems as if every year there are more students with learning disabilities in my classes. Is the number of students with learning disabilities really going up?*

Melanie: Over the past 10 to 20 years, the K-12 educational system has improved identification of many types of disabilities, including learning disabilities, attention-deficit/hyperactivity disorder, and psychiatric/psychological disorders. National statistics show that 11 percent of postsecondary students experience a disability (National Center for Education Statistics, 2006). According to other sources, this number has nearly doubled between the academic year 1999–2000 and the academic year 2007–2008.

Reprinted from *The Teaching Professor,* May 2010

Universal Design: What, How, and Why?

Patty Kohler-Evans and Candice Dowd Barnes

Universal Design for Learning (UDL) grew out of the work of Ron Mace, an architect in the 1980s, who avidly advocated for individuals with disabilities. Mace made it his life's purpose to ensure that products and environments were usable by everyone. For example, we have all used and benefited from the curb cut. Dragging a baby stroller up a step sometimes takes the help of a benevolent stranger, when a simple slope in the concrete facilitates travel for everyone. Curb cuts were primarily for individuals in wheelchairs, but they also work for adults with shopping carts, rolling luggage, or baby strollers, and even for children on bicycles! In more recent years, this concept of universal design has been applied to our profession as a way to help all students access learning. UDL is guided by three key principles: providing multiple means of representation, the "what" of learning; providing multiple means of action and expression, the "how" of learning; and providing multiple means of engagement, the "why" of learning. We would like to briefly explore each of these principles and offer some suggestions for making UDL work in the university classroom.

What: providing multiple means of representation

When UDL is applied to the university classroom, we must consider the many ways our students access information; this is the "what" of learning. Gone are the days when we can simply stand and dispense our knowledge. We have students with sensory issues, such as blindness or deafness; we have students with learning disabilities such as dyslexia; and we have students with language differences, to name a few. How do we make sure they can access our content? For starters, we can incorporate multiple modalities—vision, hearing, and touch. When we prepare, we should be asking ourselves if our presentation will be accessible to everyone or if it's just the way we are used to delivering content. We can adapt our format by ampli-fying sound or providing captions, enlarging our text, changing the font, or even using color to emphasize major points. We can provide hands-on experiences using models or manipulatives. We should also carefully exam-ine our use of various types of language, symbols, or expressions, and work to connect our content to students' previous experiences. The use of tables, videos, animation, and even comic strips can enhance the meaning of our content.

How: providing multiple means of action and expression

The second principle refers to the "how" of learning. How do we en-sure that our students convey to us what they are learning? Students should be given the opportunity to represent what they know in a variety of ways. For instance, some may need to verbally express their understanding, while others may need to write what they have learned. We have students with physical challenges, and for them, using alternatives to pen and pencil or even a mouse may be indicated. Thankfully, technological advances have provided us with such tools as joysticks and voice-activated programs or switches. Multiple media may help some candidates; film, music, dance, or other forms of movement can also be ways of communicating what has been learned. Other means of expression include interactive Web tools or social media. Software programs such as those designed to check spelling or grammar, predict words, or convert text to speech should be options. Some students may need additional support in the form of scaffolded instruction, checklists, or schedules that help them successfully manage their learning.

Why: providing multiple means of engagement

The third principle focuses on the "why" of learning. Here, our atten-tion turns to factors such as background knowledge, culture, and personal relevance, which are different for every student. What can we offer that will enhance the engagement of everyone? We can start by thinking about students' interests. We can cultivate engagement by offering different ways to reach course objectives and individual academic goals. When we provide a safe environment that encourages self-expression and connects with our students' personal lives and other characteristics, we increase the likelihood that learning will take place and that engagement will grow. Students vary in their possession of motivation and self-regulation skills. We increase their likelihood of success when we show them how to break large tasks into manageable parts. Peer groups, mentors, and coaches can also provide sup-port that increases engagement with course content and activities.

Final thoughts

When viewed collectively, UDL means that information is presented in a flexible manner, taking into account how students may best express their learning and how they are best engaged in their learning tasks. In short, all students deserve access to the curriculum in ways that make the learning meaningful to them.

Reprinted from *The Teaching Professor,* June 2014

The Imposter with the Roster: How I Gave up Control and Became a Better Teacher

Keith Starcher

By the spring of 2008, I had been a full-time professor for seven years and had learned (I thought) a great deal about becoming more of a "guide on the side." But now I was at a different school and facing senior students in an advertising and promotions class. I had never taught advertising and promotions before. My marketing courses to date had all focused on strategy, market research, data analysis—I'm Mr. Logic, not Mr. Creative.

For the first time in my short-lived teaching career (after a somewhat longer career in business), I felt more like an "imposter with a roster." These students wanted to learn the creative aspects of advertising as well as advertising strategy. I could only offer them the latter. The students and I suffered through the semester together. My end-of-course evaluations were terrible—and I knew I deserved them. I was humiliated and discouraged. What could I do?

Spring semester, 2010—the dreaded advertising and promotions course reared its ugly head again. But this time, things would be different. Why—*because I was different*. I was determined to do whatever it took to make that horrendous course a blessing to both me and my students. It took months, but I finally found a textbook that would help me guide the students through the advertising creative process. My plan was to use this textbook and give much of the control of the class to the 16 seniors enrolled in the course. I was up front with them about my lack of expertise in the creative marketing area. I laid out some objectives for advertising strategy and the creative aspects of advertising, but then I asked the class how we might reach those objectives, which assessments to use, what the semester-long project should look like, the timing of the major submissions for the class, etc. I am pleased to report that what we decided as a group was no less rigorous than what I would have planned for a course at this level.

After we laid out the semester calendar, the students and I really began working together. There were classes in which I lectured, but the majority of our classes were led by individual students helping their peers complete exercises from the textbook, or giving feedback on the various creative advertising projects the students were working on. I also invited several guests to our class who had much more experience than I in the world of advertising. They were well received by the students.

At semester's end, although the final grade distribution was not significantly different from that of my other classes, my student ratings were stellar (the highest of any class that I've ever taught). I was further encouraged by comments like these: "I love how the semester went, I was honestly a little hesitant to like the fact that students would be 'teaching' a lot of the time, but now I'm glad it worked out that way." And, "I think advertising in real life is a mix of principles and application, which is exactly what we received this semester—principles from the book (one of the best textbooks I've ever read) and application from class work."

What was different in this course in 2010 compared to the course in 2008?

- From prior classes, I had developed a relationship with these students. These students trusted me.
- Although the students knew that I had high academic standards, they also appreciated my willingness to give up more than just a little control of the class—to work outside my comfort zone for their benefit.
- I selected a great textbook for what I hoped to accomplish in this course.

Do I plan to follow this methodology in my other classes? My first response is "No." But a colleague suggested that I reconsider. Why not give up a little control to beginning students? And so, with a little trepidation, this fall I plan to trust my freshmen students by allowing them to help me with a few classroom policies—maybe even alter the design of some of their assessments. I'm eager to continue my journey from "imposter with a roster" to "first among peers" as my students and I create a dynamic learning community both inside and outside the classroom.

Reprinted from *The Teaching Professor*, October 2010

About the Contributors

Kenneth L. Alford, PhD, is a professor of church history and doctrine at Brigham Young University. After serving almost 30 years on active duty in the U.S. Army, he retired as a Colonel in 2008. Alford served in numerous assignments while on active military duty, including the Pentagon, eight years teaching computer science at the United States Military Academy at West Point, and four years as department chair and professor teaching strategic leadership at the National Defense University in Washington, DC. He has published and presented on a wide variety of topics during his career.

Laurie Bjerklie, MA, MLS, is the medical laboratory technician program coordinator at Rasmussen College–Moorhead. She is passionate about higher education and teaching our next generations along with mentoring faculty. Bjerklie is a forward thinker and supporter of simulation in education. At Rasmussen College, she has developed course curriculum and assessments for all MLT residential programmatic classes. Bjerklie got her BS in clinical laboratory science from The University of North Dakota and MA in curriculum and instruction from Saint Xavier University.

Kevin Brown, PhD, is a professor of English in the department of language and literature at Lee University. He has published three full-length collections of poems: *Liturgical Calendar: Poems* (2014), *A Lexicon of Lost Words* (2013; Winner of the Violet Reed Haas Prize for Poetry), and *Exit Lines* (2009). He has also published a scholarly work, *They Love to Tell the Story: Five Contemporary Authors Take on the Gospels* (2012) with Kennesaw State University press. Brown is the only member of Lee's faculty ever to be awarded each of three major faculty awards: Excellence in Advising ('10), Excellence in Scholarship ('11), and Excellence in Teaching ('12).

Amy Burden, MATL, is an instructor in the department of modern languages at Mississippi College. She is also a doctoral student in applied linguistics at the University of Memphis. Her research interests include technology-enhanced language learning (TELL) and peace education and linguistics.

Anna Butler is professor of mathematics in the department of mathematics at Polk State College, Lakeland, FL.

Sarah K. Clark, PhD, is an assistant professor of elementary education in the school of teacher education and leadership at Utah State University. She has been honored with the Jerry Johns Promising Researcher Award in 2013 for her work on literacy. Clark got her MA in education with specialization in language, reading, and culture, and PhD in curriculum and instruction with specialization in literacy and teacher education from the Utah State University.

Lisa M. Shappee is the library director and instructional designer for Kansas State University Polytechnic. Shappee received her Master of Library Science and MS in instructional technology and design from Emporia State University. She has presented regionally, nationally and internationally on faculty development, distance education and instructional technology. Shappee is responsible for creating online teaching training as well as faculty technology training on the K-State Polytechnic Campus.

John A. Dern is an associate professor of instruction in the Intellectual Heritage Program at Temple University in Philadelphia. He earned his PhD in English from Lehigh University. A teacher since 1991, he received the 2009 Violet B. Ketels Award for teaching from the Intellectual Heritage Program and the 2017 College of Liberal Arts Teaching/Instructional Faculty Award. He has published one book, *Martians, Monsters and Madonna: Fiction and Form in the World of Martin Amis*, and essays on a variety of subjects.

Rob Dornsife, PhD, is a professor of English and director of the writing center at Creighton University. Dornsife received Creighton University's highest student-selected teaching honor, the Robert F. Kennedy Student Award for Excellence in Teaching, and the Creighton College of Arts and Sciences the College Award for Professional Excellence in Full Time Teaching. He also won a Reloy Garcia Award for Excellence in Teaching in English. Creighton's campus newspaper, *The Creightonian*, cited Rob (in a tie) as "favorite professor" in its "Best of CU" supplement.

Candice Dowd Barnes is an associate professor at the University of Central Arkansas in the department of elementary, literacy and special education. She is also the chief operations officer for Parker Education & Development, LLC. Barnes strongly believes in the power of authentic learning experiences to teach beyond the walls of the classroom into all aspects of life. Barnes has an extensive background in early childhood education, curriculum and assessment planning, and educational leadership.

Karen Eifler is the co-director of the Garaventa Center for Catholic Intellectual Life and American Culture and professor in the School of Education at University of Portland. She is co-founder of the University's Faith and Intellectual Life Group, a creative faculty and staff seminar for spiritual and spirited debate. Eifler is widely published in her field and has earned several academic awards in recent years, including the first national Collegium Visionary Award in 2014, University of Portland's Culligan Medal for Faculty Service in 2014, Deans' Award for Faculty Leadership and Outstanding Teaching in 2000.

Melanie Gangle is the program manager for Accessible Education Services at the University of Portland. She got her MS in education, rehabilitation counseling from Western Oregon University.

Krista Greear is the assistant director for disability resources for students, a division of student life, at the University of Washington where she manages the access text and technology program and captioning program for all three UW campuses. She is involved with the UW's web council, approaches on accessibility interest group, online advising group and husky toastmasters.

Jim Guinee, PhD, is a licensed psychologist who obtained his bachelor's in psychology and doctorate in counseling psychology from the University of Illinois. In addition to training and supervision, his clinical interests include relationship issues, couples counseling, grief and loss, dream interpretation, and religious/spiritual issues. He also serves as the adjunct faculty of family and consumer sciences.

John Hilton III is an assistant professor of Ancient Scripture. Prior to coming to BYU, he worked with the LDS Seminary and Institute program for 11 years in a variety of capacities. Hilton has a PhD in instructional psychology and technology from BYU. He loves to teach, and his research focuses on issues relating to both religious pedagogy and open educational resources.

Grace Johnson is a McCoy Professor and the lead instructor for the accounting and public accounting majors. As well as teaching financial accounting, she is responsible for courses in accounting information systems, accounting research, business ethics, and international business. Johnson has published four textbooks, and is an active presenter at accounting and international business conferences. She has taught in Brazil, China, and South Korea, and recently returned from sabbatical research undertaken in Finland and Poland. Current research interests include studies of internal control and corporate governance, data analytics in the accounting curriculum, cloud computing use among municipal finance offices, and trust repair after C-suite scandals. Among Johnson's recent publications are articles in the *American International Journal of Social Sciences, The Accounting Educator*, the *Journal of Government Financial Management,* and the *ISACA Journal.*

Patricia Kohler-Evans, EdD, is a professor at the University of Central Arkansas in the department of elementary, literacy, and special education. She also serves as the director of the UCA Mashburn Center for Learning. As a former teacher, she has worked with students with disabilities for over 30 years. She has also published numerous articles on co-teaching, the importance of developing positive relationships with students as well as teachers. Kohler-Evans also serves as an executive coach for the Little Rock School District.

Patrick R. Lowenthal is an associate professor at Boise State University, where he teaches master's and doctoral students in fully online graduate programs. He researches how people communicate using emerging technologies—with a specific focus on issues of presence, identity, and community online.

Carol Martinson, MEd, is a professor of English and first year experience at Polk State College. She has been an educator for 25 years, having taught middle and high school, as well as college. She earned a Bachelor of Science degree in education from Slippery Rock University of Pennsylvania, a Master of Education with a concentration in English and reading from the University of South Carolina, and has completed coursework toward a teaching in higher education doctorate at Florida International University.

Laura Mastel, MA, MLS (ASCP)[CM], currently works as a microbiologist and facilitates on-the-bench instruction of medical laboratory students. She is committed to sharing on the job best practices and giving her students quality hands-on experience. She also teaches as an online adjunct instructor for various colleges. She received her BS in Clinical Laboratory Science from the University of North Dakota and MA in Curriculum and Instruction from Saint Xavier University.

Michelle D. Miller, PhD, is director of the First Year Learning Initiative, professor of psychological sciences, and president's distinguished teaching fellow at Northern Arizona University. Miller co-created the First Year Learning Initiative at Northern Arizona University and is active in course redesign, serving as a redesign scholar for the National Center for Academic Transformation. She is the author of *Minds Online: Teaching Effectively with Technology* (Harvard University Press, 2014), and has written about evidence-based pedagogy in scholarly as well as general-interest publications.

John Orlando serves as the associate director of the faculty resource center at Northcentral University. He is currently the editor of *Online Class-room* newsletter and has written numerous articles on teaching and learning, including the "Online Learning 2.0" column for the newsletter. Orlando has published over 75 articles and delivered over 50 presentations, workshops, and keynotes on online education, teaching with technology, and social media. He is a passionate education consultant, educator, and educational administrator helping teachers learn how to use online, Web 2.0, and other technologies to transform their teaching practice and improve student performance.

Keith Starcher is a professor in the division of business at Indiana Wesleyan University. Starcher has more than 30 years of business experience. After graduating with a degree in metallurgy from Penn State, he continued his graduate studies at the University of South Florida obtaining both an MBA and a PhD. He is interested in the scholarship of teaching and learning; in particular, how SoTL applies to the part-time, online instructor. Starcher got his PhD and MBA both from the University of South Florida and MDiv from the Trinity Theological Seminary.

Susan Taylor is the Montine McDaniel Freeman director of the New Orleans Museum of Art (NOMA). She holds art history degrees from Vassar College and the Institute of Fine Arts at New York University.

Courtlann Thomas, PhD, is the director of Teaching Learning Computing Center (TLCC) and Learning Resources at the Polk State College, Lakeland, FL. She has 20 years of academic administrative and teaching experience in libraries, teaching/learning support centers (tutoring/testing), and faculty development. Thomas got her Master of Library and Information Science from the University of Tennessee-Knoxville and PhD in education from the Capella University.

Dale Tracy, PhD, is a determinate assistant professor in the department of English at the Royal Military College of Canada. She has research interests in humor, autobiography, poetry, and performance. Her articles are forthcoming or available in *Popular Music, English Studies in Canada, MaComère, Mosaic, Canadian Literature*, and *Modern Drama*. She is the author of *With the Witnesses: Poetry, Compassion, and Claimed Experience* (McGill-Queen's, 2017).

Jennifer Waldeck, PhD, is associate professor in the School of Communication at Chapman University, where she is director of the graduate teaching associate and basic communication curriculum programs. Waldeck is the author or co-author of several books, including *Communication Competence: Goals and Contexts* (Bridgepoint Publishing). Waldeck is on the Teaching Professor Conference advisory board and served as the 2017 (St. Louis) Conference Chair. She regularly contributes blogs and newsletter columns for Magna Publications, including *Faculty Focus* and *The Teaching Professor* newsletter.

Maryellen Weimer, PhD, has been the guiding hand and constant voice behind *The Teaching Professor* newsletter since 1987. She is an award-winning professor emerita of teaching and learning at Penn State Berks and won Penn State's Milton S. Eisenhower award for distinguished teaching in 2005. She has published several books, including *Inspired College Teaching: A Career-Long Resource for Professional Growth* (Jossey-Bass, 2010).

Lynda L. Wolverton, PhD, is the instructor and department coordinator for QEP at the Polk State College, Lakeland. She received her PhD in leadership in higher education from the Capella University.

Additional Resources
from Magna Publications

BULK PURCHASES

To purchase multiple print copies of this book, please visit:
www.MagnaGroupBooks.com

MEMBERSHIPS/SUBSCRIPTIONS

Faculty Focus
www.facultyfocus.com
A free e-newsletter on effective teaching strategies for the college classroom.

The Teaching Professor Membership
www.TeachingProfessor.com
The Teaching Professor is an annual membership that reflects the changing needs of today's college faculty and the students they teach. This new fully online version of the newsletter that faculty have enjoyed for more than 30 years includes the best of the print version—great articles and practical, evidence-based insights—but also many new features including video, graphics, and links that make it an even more indispensable resource.

Academic Leader Membership
www.Academic-Leader.com
Academic Leader covers the trends, challenges, and best practices today's academic decision-makers. Members gain access to the latest thinking in academic leadership and learn how peers at other institutions are solving problems, managing change, and setting direction. New articles are published throughout the month.

CONFERENCES

The Teaching Professor Annual Conference
www.TeachingProfessorConference.com
This event provides an opportunity to learn effective pedagogical techniques, hear from leading teaching experts, and interact with colleagues committed to teaching and learning excellence. Join more than 1,000 educators from around the country.

Leadership in Higher Education Conference
www.AcademicLeadershipConference.com
The Leadership in Higher Education Conference provides higher-education leaders with an opportunity to expand leadership skills with proactive strategies, engaging networking, time-saving tips, and best practices. Attendees will hear from a roster of prestigious experts and nationally recognized thought leaders. A broad mix of plenary addresses, concurrent sessions, and timely roundtable discussions leave no topic untouched.

BOOKS

The Academic Leader's Handbook: A Resource Collection for College Administrators
https://www.amazon.com/dp/B0764KMC5Z
The Academic Leader's Handbook: A Resource Collection for College Administrators details an array of proven management strategies and will help further your achievements as a leader in higher education. Discover new leadership tools and insights at departmental, administrative, and executive levels.

Active Learning: A Practical Guide for College Faculty
https://www.amazon.com/dp/B071ZN8R32
Learn how to apply active learning methods in both small and large classes as well as in an online teaching environment. Whether you are new to active learning methods or experienced with them, this comprehensive reference book can guide you every step of the way.

Essential Teaching Principles: A Resource Collection for Adjunct Faculty
https://www.amazon.com/dp/0912150246
This book provides a wealth of both research-driven and classroom-tested best practices to help adjuncts develop the knowledge and skills required to run a successful classroom. Compact and reader-friendly, this book is conveniently organized to serve as a ready reference whenever a new teaching challenge arises—whether it's refreshing older course design, overcoming a student's objection to a grade, or fine-tuning assessments.

Essential Teaching Principles: A Resource Collection for Teachers
https://www.amazon.com/dp/0912150580
This book serves as a quick and ready reference as you encounter the challenges of teaching college-level material in the high school classroom. For an AP or IB teacher, there's no better resource.

Faculty Development: A Resource Collection for Academic Leaders
https://www.amazon.com/dp/0912150661
Discover proven tips and insights, from top academic experts, that will help you enhance faculty development programming and training on your campus.

Flipping the College Classroom: Practical Advice from Faculty
https://www.amazon.com/dp/B01N2GZ61O
This collection is a comprehensive guide to flipping no matter how much—or how little—experience you have with it. If you are just getting started, you will learn where and how to begin. If you have been at it for a while, you will find new ideas to try and solutions to common challenges. Flipping the College Classroom: Practical Advice from Faculty is an invaluable resource that covers all the necessary territory.

Grading Strategies for the Online College Classroom: A Collection of Articles for Faculty
https://www.amazon.com/dp/0912150564

Do your grading practices accurately reflect your online students' performance? Do your assessment and feedback methods inspire learning? Are you managing the time you spend on these things—or is the workload overwhelming? *Grading Strategies for the Online College Classroom: A Collection of Articles for Faculty* can help you master the techniques of effective online grading—while avoiding some of the more costly pitfalls.

Helping Students Learn: Resources, Tools, and Activities for College Educators
https://www.amazon.com/dp/0912150602

This collection is packed with ideas, strategies, resources, activities, assignments, handouts, and more for teachers to use in the classroom to help their students become better at the very thing they are there to do: Learn.

Features of the book include: summaries of current research (with full citations); assignments or quizzes to use in the classroom; handouts to distribute to students; review and reflection worksheets at the end of every section; and thoughts and reflections from Maryellen Weimer.

Managing Adjunct Faculty: A Resource Collection for Administrators
https://www.amazon.com/dp/B01N2OVK5W

Chances are your adjunct population has been built on an ad hoc basis to fill instructional needs. As a result, your institution might not have a solid management framework to support them. That's a gap you can close with guidance from *Managing Adjunct Faculty: A Resource Collection for Administrators*. This invaluable guide offers an extensive review of best practices for managing an adjunct cohort and integrating them more fully into your campus community.

Teaching Strategies for the Online College Classroom: A Collection of Faculty Articles
https://www.amazon.com/dp/0912150483

Includes online teaching strategies ranging from building a successful start of the semester, fostering productive connections, managing challenging behavior in the online classroom, and enhancing student engagement.

Made in the USA
Columbia, SC
24 July 2019